Imam ALI

A BEACON OF COURAGE

IMAM ALI

A BEACON OF COURAGE

SULAYMAN KATTANI

TRANSLATED BY:
I. K. A. HOWERD

with
Prefatory Remarks by
Imam Shaykh Murtaḍā Āl Yā Sīn
and Foreword by
Al-Ustādh Ja^{c}far Khalīlī

ISLAMIC EDUCATION CENTER

First published in 1983

ISBN 0 9506986 6 0

Second Printing : 1991

Islamic Education Center
7917 Montrose Road
Potomac, MD 20854

Printed and bound in Beirut - Lebanon
AL - NOUR Fundation P.O.Box : 8645/11

TRANSLITERATION

Arabic Letter	Transliteration
ء	'
ب	b
ت	t
ث	th
ج	j
ح	ḥ
خ	kh
د	d
ذ	dh
ر	r
ز	z
س	s
ش	sh
ص	ṣ
ض	ḍ
ط	ṭ
ظ	ẓ
ع	ʿ
غ	gh
ف	f
ق	q
ك	k
ل	l
م	m
ن	n
ه	h
و	w
ي	y
ة	t

Short Vowels

ـَ	a
ـُ	u
ـِ	i

Long Vowels

ـَا	ā
ـُو	ū
ـِي	ī

Diphthongs

ـَوْ	aw
ـَيْ	ay
ـِيّ	iyy
ـُوّ	uww

Introduction to the Translation

The task of translating this work has been particularly difficult. The author's approach to the life of ᶜAlī has not been along the usual biographical lines. In keeping with the literary competition which the book was written for, the language is picturesque and highly literary. The whole tenor and style of the treatment of Imam ᶜAlī serves to give an insight into his character rather than to present an historical account. Historical incidents are used as vehicles for this purpose. The result is very effective in Arabic but it has presented great problems in trying to translate not just the language, but the images from one language to the other.

Despite this difficulty, the translation has been particularly rewarding for it has introduced a new dimension for my understanding of Imam ᶜAlī. It makes it possible to escape from the mere historical enumeration of the details of the life of a great figure in Islamic history and to gain some appreciation of the inner meaning of the man in the understanding of the Arabs. The religious and literary influence of ᶜAlī has long been recognised by scholarship but rarely is that influence demonstrated in a work published in the West. I hope that his translation may be a small contribution towards our understanding of that influence.

The author is an Arab Christian from Lebanon and his work can, in some ways, be described as a helpful advance in Muslim-Christian relations. In his work we see a Christian's view of the wonderful nature and religious temperament of Imam ᶜAlī. This attempt to portray a great Muslim Imam may help to lead to a greater understanding of the religious truths of Islam.

The text used for translation is the text of 1st edition in 1966, published in Najaf. In the translation Qur'ānic quotations have been referred to by giving the number of the *sura* in Roman numerals and the verses in ordinary numerals.

Finally, I would like to thank the Muḥammādi Trust for making this translation possible.

May 1st, 1983

I. K. A. Howard
University of Edinburgh

In Memory of
Muḥammad Reza ᶜAlī Sayeed

CONTENTS

PREFATORY REMARKS

His Eminence Imam Shaykh Murtaḍā Āl Yā Sīn, President of the group of scholars at Najaf and Chairman of the Committee of the Writing Competition, has graciously given this blessed message.

In the Name of God, the Merciful and the Compassionate.

Praise be to God and may God bless Muḥammad and his family.

God, may His power be exalted, has wanted to make clear the way for the one who brought this book from the domain of the heart to the domain of the pen, and provided ways and means for it to be printed easily so that it may come before the people as a book which openly reveals what is right and speaks the truth. Thus the ignorant may derive knowledge from it and those who know may gain from its style and prose. Such is its quality that by its pure style – the least which can be said of that is that it is a style of unprecedented clarity, which contains ornate expressions and special meaning – it presents something which is worthy of all admiration and appreciation.

Perhaps in its oratorical style it is the first book on its subjects which has brought interwoven into its personality an image of *Nahj al-Balāgha*. Therefore thanks are due to the author, the man of knowledge, from every friend of Imam ʿAli, peace be on him. Thanks are also due to those good men of learning. who have prepared the way to make possible the production of such a unique book as this and for the other books which share its subject. Of these men mention should especially be made of the two noble Sayyids, the august and eloquent preacher al Sayyid Jawād Shubar, whose much appreciated efforts had the greatest influence on the success of this writing competition and the noble and praiseworthy a Sayyid Hāshim Shubar, who donated from his private wealth all the three prizes which were distributed to the three winners. I hope that this intellectual literary competition which has achieved this valuable result will open the door to further competitions which will provide Islamic libraries with precious books like these or even better. That is something which would be possible for thinkers and writers but God is the One from Whom help should be sought and He is the Provider of success.

FOREWORD

By al-Ustādh Ja^cfar al-Khalīlī

I

For fourteen centuries, the name of Imam ᶜAlī has occupied the first place in the studies of historians, scholars and researchers whenever mention has been made of faith, rectitude, justice, bravery, struggle on the path of God and endurance in the face of adversities, or when there is any discussion of knowledge, wisdom, literature, poetry and oratory. Thus the story of his life has continued to be reported in pictures which have been coloured by qualities never before united in the personality of one gifted genius as they have been united in this wonderful unique personality which has captivated the minds of men and bewildered their intellects. These qualities were so strong and firm from the point of view of knowledge, wisdom, understanding, and moral values of true humanity, that they swept away the adversities (whose concern was to destroy anything, however great), whenever these adversities stood before them.

Ḍirār b. Ḍamira al-Kinānī, a contemporary of ᶜAlī at the time, said, when Muᶜāwiya forced him to say what he thought about ᶜAlī: "By God, he was vast in stature, great in strength. He had the last word on any subject. He judged with justice. Knowledge sprung forth from his both sides. Wisdom came from every aspect of him. He kept away from the splendours of the world and befriended the loneliness of the night. He was full of tears for men and thought much. Rough clothes and coarse food were enough for him. He was among us like one of us. He was amenable to us when we came to him. He answered us when we questioned him. By God, when he was close to us and near to us, we would hardly dare speak to him out of awe of him. Yet he magnified men of religion and brought the poor close to him. The strong could not exploit his lack of means and the weak did not despair of his justice."

ᶜAlī was like an independent believing community in its very essence, which speaks with the rationality of time and expresses the maturity of time and gives form to the final stages of the ascent of man and the summit of glory. It is not right for ᶜAlī to be compared with other individuals, for he is only of such texture. It is wrong for it to be said of ʿAlī that he was the most outstanding, the most God-fearing, the noblest and the most generous of men while you examine the lives and human qualities of great men. Just as it is not possible for you to compare the splendour of the earth with the moon in its quality of brilliancy or to compare radium with other minerals in essence. So it is not possible for you to compare the name of ʿAlī with the names of great men – with the exception of those who attained the rank of prophethood and, of course, he is not a prophet – because the qualities of ʿAlī transcend usual limits and because his personality has attained the summit of glory and the highest ideal in the world of men.

When man seeks to examine principles, skill and qualities it is not right for him to take ʿAlī as an example. That is because ʿAlī is, as I have said, like an independent community whose like does not exist among ordinary individuals. He has risen above men through the excellencies which he brought, the qualities he made manifest and the characteristics of the unequalled perfect man which were given expression through him. Thus the word "ʿAlī" alone is sufficient to draw before the eye all the magnetic pictures involved in the essential element of humanity.

Perhaps the word "ʿAlī", which some write above their shops and stores or hang on artistic boards engraved on their walls, or which they carve on the doors of buildings, mosques, institutes and foundations, perhaps this word is a kind of eloquence and a well-known technical symbol in the art of eloquence for self-sufficiency. It is pure in pronounciation and clear in understanding. There is no need for anything to be added for people to understand that ʿAlī conveys the perfect gathering in of the fine virtues and qualities of the world.

As Mahdī al-Jawāhirī has said:

"Enumeration of a man's good attributes is to fail him when his good attributes transcend enumeration."

And the qualities of ʿAlī exceed the bounds of enumeration and challenge the factors of time which drive the past and present before them and which tries to destroy them completely. But the qualities of ʿAlī challenged the factors of time with a power whose equal has not been known in the history of great men so that his personality became like the sun which, whenever the mists or clouds or dust hide it or the moon comes between it and the earth, they cannot hide it for ever, nor are they strong enough to change its essence and the power of its work and its effect on earth and nature.

II

I mean by the factors of time and the active forces, such as the awakening of desire which includes techniques of propaganda and the winning over of men by promises, generosity and gifts which were among the things used by the enemies of ʿAlī in every form and kind to bring down a veil over his merits, to hide them from the eyes of men and to remove them from the register of existence.

I mean by the factors of time and the active forces, such as intimidation which includes threats, menaces, prison, banishment and murder in its most dreadful forms to wipe out any remaining trace of ʿAlī, his sons and friends who were among those who still look to ʿAlī and his righteous offspring for some sanctity and love in their lives.

Whenever the combination of awakening desire and intimidation takes place in all its hideous forms and techniques, it is easy for the one in whose hands are these two real forces to change the direction of men's thought, to change beliefs and to lay a thick curtain over the past with regard to all its qualities and virtues and the factors which make a man believe in it and adhere to its principles.

The awakening of desire alone is today considered one of the most effective weapons of war and one of the most destructive. Then how much more powerful will it be if elements of intimidation are joined to it. Extensive propaganda has been exercised today on researchers and historians about the reality of affairs so that they do not know – for example – whether Germany was in reality the greatest cause of the first and second wars or whether it was England who did not want anyone to touch the least of its rights in the colonies.

From our readings, we have seen how the combination of the awakening of desire and intimidation works, how it changes the basic dispositions in nations, how it changes the tendencies and beliefs of people to things which contradict those tendencies and beliefs. It was something of that which enabled the Ayyūbids to change Egypt from being Shīʿite in its basic belief to being an Egypt which was Sunnī. It enabled the Safāwids to change Iran which was Sunnī in origin and belief into Shīʿite Iran. In both cases the Ayyūbids and the Safāwids used the techniques of awakening desire and intimidation which included eradication of a belief and the complete transplanting of a contradictory belief in its place.

The story of Edward VIII is not too far distant from the minds of men. It will serve as evidence of the manner of how the people abandoned him and forgot about him almost between evening and morning, merely by the government removing his pictures from the walls and forbidding the newspapers to repeat his name and mention any news about him. Yet, before, their minds had been full of him and their hearts had been full of love and loyalty for him. Soon, only a few knew where he lived and how he lived, this loved and respected king of yesterday! This is the case when propaganda has not gone beyond simple primitive levels.

Ibn Abī al-Ḥadīd, the author of the famous commentary on *Nahj al-Balāgha*, says: ʿAṭā' reported on the authority of ʿAbd Allāh b. Shaddād b. al-Hād who said: "If the stories reported about the merit of ʿAlī had not been so famous, so profuse and so numerously reported, their reporting would have been stopped out of fear of the Umayyads because of the intensity of their enmity towards him. If it had not been for the fact that God, the Exalted, had some hidden purpose known by those given knowledge of it, in continuation of ʿAlī's name, no story would have been reported about his virtues and none of his virtues would have been known. Don't you see that if the leader of a village is angry with one of the inhabitants and prevents the people from mentioning any good about him, he would become unknown, his name forgotten and he would become, while still existing, non-existent, while still alive, dead?"

III

The Awakening of Desire

Those factors and means, the means of awakening desire and intimidation, were used in the different forms and aspects against ʿAlī and his sons after him. This hostility continued to march along with time into history despite the progress of science, the spread of culture and the development of men's ability to discuss, study, investigate and to reject fanaticism. Right up until today, there are still those who hate ʿAlī, who revile him and curse him. Yet more than thirteen centuries have passed since the martyrdom and death of ʿAlī and we still hear the voice of ʿImrān b. Ḥaṭṭān al-Raqqāshī – he was the man who venerated ʿAbd al-Raḥmān b. Muljam and praised the blow which ʿAbd al-Raḥmān b. Muljam struck against the head of Imam ʿAlī – when he said:

> O blow of a pious man, by which he wants nothing but to reach Paradise near the throne of God.
>
> I remember him today and I count him the most faithful of creatures in the balance of judgement by God.[1]

When Ben Bella, the Algerian leader, visited Iraq the first thing he asked about was him. He asked about the tomb of ᶜAbd al-Raḥmān b. Muljam or the place of his death. He showed his wish to visit it and to recite the Opening Sūra of the Qur'ān over it . . . There have occurred those who have neatly dismissed such a question as this and have pointed to it in terms of one of the requirements of policy which had to be made allowances for on this visit. Even if this story of Ben Bella is not true, it is, nevertheless, true of not a few people who still, even today, curse ᶜAlī and ask for mercy for his killer, ᶜAbd al-Raḥmān b. Muljam.

We say that every means of awakening desire and intimidation has been used to eradicate the name of ᶜAlī and his merit. Every useful means, great or small, have been adopted to attain this end. Yet, these means with all the power, force and influence they contain and even with their perfect preparation and enforcement at the hands of skillful enemies with experience and wordly wisdom have been no more capable than have the thin webs of the spiders been able to bind the necks of lions and drag them where they want. Thus the memory of ᶜAlī and his righteous sons has emerged more clearly, more understood and more real after those attempts which even Satan has been weaving in all the kinds of awakening of desire and intimidation.

It is true that persecution may help preserve adherence to the opposite view and to the belief which is opposed to the belief of the persecutor and make it more deeply-rooted in the mind. However, persecution accompanied by the awakening of desire and good propaganda will never produce the reaction on such a scale which accompanied the reaction of those who were persecuted for ᶜAlī, and his sons and his Shīᶜa. Among their effects were the emergence of the extremists, those who made ᶜAlī into a God, and who associated with him every miracle which the mind could not even grant to the prophets, let alone the successors of prophets. These effects caused the name of ᶜAlī to be mentioned in the "call for the prayer" of the Shīᶜa and thus to be associated with their prayers as a reaction to the cursing which the enemies of ᶜAlī required of themselves before and after prayer and when supplicating God. It has been reported and Ibn Abī al-Ḥadīd has mentioned:

"Mu^cāwiya, ^cAmr b. al-Aṣ, al-Maghīra b. Shu^cba, al-Walīd b. ^cUqba, Abu al-A^cwar, al-Ḍaḥḥak b. Qays, Busr b. Arṭa'a, Ḥabīb b. Maslama, Abū Mūsā al-Ash^carī and Marwān b. al-Ḥakam, all used to make a petition in the prayer and curse ^cAlī."

This is evidence for the greatness of ^cAlī, a greatness as a result of which the personality of ^cAlī has remained for fourteen centuries and will continue for tens and hundreds of centuries just as if it were a great new personality unknown to authors, historians and students of biography which has no like in the history of man.

The enemies of ^cAlī perfected the form of the propaganda and the means of awakening desire against ^cAlī so that many believe their statements. Many of the people were an ignorant rabble for whom it did not require much effort to change their opinion and lead them astray for those who knew the methods and techniques of propaganda and who are characterised by knowing how to manage things. Anyone who makes a thorough study of Islamic history will see the good fortune of the leaders of the enemies of ^cAlī in understanding propaganda and the methods and the ways of awakening desire. The guarantee of its effect on the men was great and especially great in view of the number of naive people there were. People, who were not familiar with cities and who did not know anything about civilisation, were not few amid such circumstances and conditions. This propaganda and the operation of awakening desire on such minds in which ignorance prevailed, worked marvellously.

Al-Mas^cūdī bears witness to the stupidity of a group of these naive people who were exploited by Umayyad propaganda, when he reports: Among his decisions of policy (i.e. the decisions of Mu^cāwiya), his perfection of them and his ability to attract the hearts of his own followers and the general people, there has been handed down the story that a man from Kūfa entered Damascus on his camel at the time of their departure from Ṣiffīn. A man from Damascus caught hold of it and said: "This is my she-camel which was taken from me at Ṣiffīn".

The dispute of the two men was brought before Mu^cāwiya. The man from Damascus produced fifty men who gave testimony that it was his she-camel. So Mu^cāwiya gave judgement against the Kūfan and ordered him to hand over the camel to the man from Damascus.

"May God restore you", the Kūfan said, "it is a male camel, not a she-camel."

"This is a decision which has already taken place", replied

Muᶜāwiya.

Then he secretly contacted the Kūfan after they had departed and had him brought to him. He asked him about the value of his camel and paid him more than the value and treated him well. Then he said: "Tell ᶜAlī I will meet him with a hundred thousand men who will not have among them any who can distinguish a she-camel from a male camel."[2]

Although this story is one of those about whose truth there can be some dispute, there is no doubt that it is a true reflection of the circumstances, the environment and the method characteristic of Muᶜāwiya, the enemies of ᶜAlī and many of the people, all of which has made possible for such stories to be attributed to them.

The enemies of ᶜAlī and of his sons, while being the source of power and authority and while having power in their hands, have been able to mobilise all the means of propaganda to raise in the minds of their subjects – the majority of whom were naive and ignorant – a general resentment against ᶜAlī and his sons. This general resentment is not public opinion as defined by sociologists.

Dr. ᶜAbd al-Laṭīf Ḥamza says: "Here it is appropriate for the researcher to distinguish clearly between two classes, at the very least, of society. The class of enlightened or cultured who are able to study affairs and the class of the mob or rabble or those who are led blindly to any view or idea, because they are completely incapable of discussing them to know how true or false they are."[3]

IV

According to this, the general resentment could in no way be termed an enlightened public opinion. History has told us of the fact that ᶜAlī's group in his own time and later times was in the vanguard in terms of behaviour, good nature, understanding, knowledge, manners and true belief. Nor was there among them any who could be described as rabble. They were three hundred and thirteen of the Emigrants and Anṣār who had fought at Badr with the Apostle. Of these, all who were still alive took part in the Battle of Ṣiffīn, fighting alongside ᶜAlī. Their number was one hundred and seventy-eight. Some sixty-three of them died as martyrs. Similarly, eight hundred of the men who had given the pledge of Raḍwān to the Prophet, under the tree at Ḥudaybiyya, and still remained alive, took part with ᶜAlī in the Battle of Ṣiffīn.[4]

These were from the believing class and the leaders of Islam and the signposts of guidance. They were those who made up really logical public opinion which represents the side of goodness, truth and righteousness. If the matter had been left to take its natural course and if the enemies of ᶜAlī had not used devilish methods and stirred up the rabble by attempting to use the means of awakening desire in order to root out the name of ᶜAlī and his sons . . . how could this not be so? Among the followers and supporters of ᶜAlī during his time were such men as Abū Dharr al-Ghiffārī, Salmān al-Fārisī, ᶜAmmār b. Yāsir, al-Miqdād, Ḥudhayfa b. al-Yamān, Khuzayma b. Thābit al-Anṣārī, Jābir al-Anṣārī, Hāshim al-Mirqāl, Muhammad b. Abī Bakr, Mālik al-Ashtar, ᶜAbd Allāh b. Masᶜūd, al-Ḥārith b. al-Nuᶜmān and hundreds of others.

As for those who took part with Muᶜāwiya in the war against ᶜAlī, all of them belonged to the Muslims who became Muslims unwillingly and were Muslims with no faith whose hearts had to be reconciled. At their head were ᶜAmr b. al-ᶜĀṣ, Abū al-Aᶜwar al-Sulamī, Busr b. Arta'a, Muslim b. ᶜUqba and others like them.[5] They are among those with whom Muᶜāwiya set out to shed blood, to spread terror and to raise general resentment and rabble-rousing.

Consciousness and understanding in lands and peoples can only be measured by a public opinion which is governed by discussion and logic. It can in no way be measured by tumult and general resentment. That is for one reason only, namely, that each one of the people in a state where a genuine public opinion prevails possesses true individuality and is able to show his true personality. He has complete freedom to explain the point of view which has convinced him and of whose correctness he wants to convince others. However, people in a state of general resentment lack their true individuality and their true nature or are very likely to. For in the crowd and the mob such qualities disappear and people think in terms of illusions and fancies. Thus there is great scope for leaders who tend to lack wisdom. Such leaders are called demagogues and they are the ones who whip up groups of people and exploit their ignorance in the absence of true individuality and natural disposition among such people.

People in a state of general agitation are something like spectators at theatre who have come under the influence of the play and what they are seeing of it. At that time they cannot make their link between what they are seeing and their critical faculties; they are unable to distinguish the variety of theatrical attitudes which are presented to them and the facts of real life.[6]

This is what, in fact, happened at the Battle of Karbalā' when the people attacked al-Ḥusayn and his followers. They were not content with killing them but they had to cut off their heads, trample with the hooves of their horses over their bodies and set fire to the tents of their womenfolk. They had to terrify their women and children, make captives of their families and with the heads of their dead ones raised on spears in front of them they marched through the town without there ever having been any crime or anything else which merited any of this.

V

It appears that the exploitation of the ingenuousness of the people to produce a general resentment and tumult, which was carried out by the enemies of ᶜAlī and of his descendants in all spheres, took place in the most skilled manner by building on the ignorance which was spread among the people. The majority were ignorant and lacked understanding so that it was easy to direct them towards the desired goal, namely to hate ᶜAlī and his descendants or at least to forget him and to forget his great qualities.

It has been reported that such was the high degree of obedience of the Syrians to Muᶜāwiya that on their way to Ṣiffīn, he performed the Friday prayer with them on Wednesday. They also accepted the statement of ᶜAmr b. al-ᶜĀṣ that it was ᶜAlī who had killed ᶜAmmār b. Yāsir, of whom the Prophet had said: "ᶜAmmār is like the skin between my eyes. Whoever is the enemy of ᶜAmmār, God is his enemy. Whoever hates ᶜAmmār, God hates him." According to ᶜAmr b. al-ᶜĀṣ, if ᶜAlī had not brought him with him to the Battle of Ṣiffīn, ᶜAmmār would not have been killed. Therefore, the curse enjoined on the killers of ᶜAmmār only referred to ᶜAlī insofar as he was the one who caused the killing and it did not refer to the actual killer, which was Muᶜāwiya or rather the soldiers of Muᶜāwiya.

Al-Masᶜūdī relates:

The matter of obedience to him – that is, obedience to Muᶜāwiya – reached such a state that they made the cursing of ᶜAlī a practice which the young were born to and the old died with. Al-Masᶜūdī added: One of the historians mentioned that he asked one of the Syrian leaders and scholars: "Who is this Abū Turāb (i.e. ᶜAlī) whom the Imam (of the prayer) curses on the pulpit?" "I think that he is a rebellious robber!" was the reply.[7]

When ᶜAbd ᶜAllāh b. ᶜAlī advanced against Marwān (the last Umayyad Caliph) in Syria, he sent to Abū al-ᶜAbbās al-Saffāḥ (the first ᶜAbbāsid Caliph) some of the leaders and men of influence in Syria. They swore to Abū al-ᶜAbbās al-Saffāḥ that they did not know about any relationship to the Prophet and the people of his household who were due his inheritance except for the Umayyads.

However, those of the enemies of ᶜAlī who were really informed were aware of his great merit and stature. Because of that, they strove with all their might to eradicate all trace of this merit and to wipe out its existence.

ᶜUmar b. ᶜAbd al-ᶜAzīz (the pious Umayyad Caliph) used to say: "When my father used to give an address and came to mention ᶜAlī – may God be pleased with him – he would stutter."

I said to him: "Father you proceed at length in your addresses, yet when you come to mention ᶜAlī, there is apparently a shortcoming in the speech."

"Have you come to notice that?" he asked.

"Yes", I replied.

"My son," he said, "if those around us knew what we know about ᶜAlī, they would desert us for his descendants."[8]

VI

The enemies of ᶜAlī varied their methods of awakening desire and propaganda, and of making up lies and fabrication and of denigrating ᶜAlī in such a way that it was difficult for anyone to believe or imagine that it would be possible for the name of ᶜAlī to arise again in the history of Islam after all those attacks and lying stories which they had tried to stick to Imam ᶜAlī. In the same way, they laid down varied firmly-set bases and plans to remove any mention of ᶜAlī, his virtues or his qualities. It came about that they would say of him things which would not even be said of evil men and criminals. It is reported on the authority of Abū Jaᶜfar (Imam Muḥammad al-Bāqir): "Muᶜāwiya set up some of the Companions and successors of the Companions to report wicked stories about ᶜAlī, peace be on him, which would make it necessary to denounce him and repudiate him. He gave them rewards to arouse their interest in such things. So they fabricated things which would please him. Among such men were Abū Hurayra, ᶜAmr b. al-ᶜĀṣ, al-Mughīra b. Shuᶜba and ᶜUrwa b. al-Zubayr.

Al-Zuhrī reported that ᶜUrwa b. al-Zubayr had told him that ᶜĀ'isha had said: I was with the Apostle of God when al-ᶜAbbās and ᶜAlī approached. "ᶜĀ'isha," he said, pointing at al-ᶜAbbās and ᶜAlī, "those two men will die outside my religion."[9]

It is reported that Muᶜāwiya gave Samara b. Jundub a hundred thousand dirhams to say that the Qurᶜānic verses (*Among men is he whose speech about the life of this world pleases you and he calls Allāh to witness as to what is in his heart, yet he is the most violent of adversaries. When he turns back, he runs along in the land that he may cause corruption in it and destroy the arable land and the stock and God does not love corruption.* II 204–5), were related about ᶜAlī. He also asked Samara to say that the noble verses (*Among men is he who sells his life out of a desire to please God.* II 207) was revealed about ᶜAbd al-Raḥmān b. Muljam. Samara would not agree to that. So he offered him two hundred thousand dirham but he still would not agree. Then he offered him four hundred thousand and he agreed.[10]

Maḥfūẓ reported: I asked Yaḥyā b. Ṣāliḥ: "You have reported on the authority of scholars like Ḥarīz, so why don't you report on the authority of Ḥarīz?".

He answered: "One day I went to him and he handed me a book. There in it was written: So-and-so reported on the authority of so-and-so that when the Prophet, may God bless him and his family, was near to death he left instructions that the hand of ᶜAlī b. Abī Ṭālib, peace be on him, should be cut off."[11]

VII

In the same way that they forged stories and traditions showing derogation of ᶜAlī and interpreted Qurᶜānic verses however they wished, they also encouraged poets to ridicule ᶜAlī and his descendants. It is not impossible that such poetry would encompass several volumes if it had not been for the fact that the historians did not bother to record it. Thus only a few examples have reached us. One such example is the poem of Kaᶜb b. Juᶜayl, in which he says:

> They say: ᶜAlī is our Imam. We say: We are satisfied with the son of Hind (muᶜāwiya). We are satisfied.
> They say: We consider that you owe allegiance to him. We say: We do not consider that we owe such allegiance.
> Before that, the thorn will be stripped of its leaves, swords will strike and spears will pierce, to the delight of our eyes.

Abū al-ᶜAbbās al-Mubarrad reported: At the end of this poem there is ridicule of ᶜAlī b. Abī Ṭālib, may God be pleased with him, that we refrain from mentioning it.[12]

Al-Mutawakkil was so violent in his perverted hatred of ᶜAlī and his descendants that he had the grave of al-Ḥusayn ploughed up and flooded with water in order to remove all traces and outlines of it. A group of men, including the poet, ᶜAlī b. al-Jahm, exploited his enmity of ᶜAlī and his descendants to the extent that before him they always referred to ᶜAlī in terms of evil and scorn, even though they had taken from ᶜAlī and his descendants what they had given them.

How true would be the two verses which ᶜAlī b. al-Jahm recited about Marwān b. Ḥafṣa for ᶜAlī b. al-Jahm himself if the ᶜAlids wished to recite them about ᶜAlī b. al-Jahm. For ᶜAlī b. al-Jahm recited about Marwān:

> The misfortune of the enmity of a man without honour and religion is not to be considered a misfortune.
> He shows you a dignity which he does not protect and he grazes away from you in your protected dignity which is protected.

Intimidation and the desire for good rewards and presents were the things which motivated the poets, the forgers of traditions and the inventors of reports so that they adopted the practice of cursing ᶜAlī as a means of gaining their sustenance and gaining high rank. If that and the propaganda had not achieved its effect on their minds, they hated ᶜAlī out of ignorance and lack of understanding. Then this hatred later changed into a principle of faith.

One day al-Ḥajjāj said: "Whoever has done a noble action, let him stand up and we will reward him for his noble action."

A man stood up and said: "Give me my reward of my hardship".

"What was your hardship?" asked al-Ḥajjāj.

"I killed al-Ḥusayn," he replied.

"How did you kill him?" al-Ḥajjāj asked.

"I struck him with my spear," he said "Then I carved into him with my sword. No one else took part in killing him with me."

"You and he will never meet in one place (i.e. Heaven)," retorted al-

Ḥajjāj and he ordered him to leave without giving him anything.[13]

On another occasion, al-Ḥajjāj spoke to ᶜAbd Allāh b. Hāni' who was a noble from the Awdaḥī tribe of Qaḥtān, who had taken part with al-Ḥajjāj in all his battles and belonged to his supporters and group. Al-Ḥajjāj wanted to reward him for all that he had done for him and show favour to his actions for him. So he said: "By God, how can I recompense you?"

Then al-Ḥajjāj forced Asmā' b. Khārija, the chief of the tribe of Fazāra, and Saᶜid b. Qays, the leader of the Yemeni tribes, to marry their two daughters to ᶜAbd Allāh b. Hāni', by threatening them with death when he saw their reluctance. Then al-Ḥajjāj said to ᶜAbd Allah b. Hāni': "Look one of your wives is the daughter of the chief of Fazāra and the other is the daughter of the chief of the tribe of Hamdān, such great men."

"May God set the governor right," replied ᶜAbd Allāh b. Hāni', "do not say that. For we have great honours which none of the Arabs have."

"What are they?," asked al-Ḥajjāj.

"Never is the Commander of the faithful ᶜAbd al-Mālik (the Umayyad Caliph) cursed in any gathering of ours," he replied.

"By God, that is a great honour," said al-Ḥajjāj.

"We took part in the battle of Ṣiffīn with the Commander of the faithful Muᶜāwiya," he said, "and not one of us fought with Abū Turāb (i.e. ᶜAlī) except for one man. By God, according to what I know of that man, he was a very evil man."

"By God, that is a great honour," said al-Ḥajjāj.

"Our women vowed that if al-Ḥusayn b. ᶜAlī was killed they would slaughter ten young camels. So they did so."

"By God, that is a great honour."

"No man of us is ever asked to curse and swear against Abū Turāb (ᶜAlī) and does so without adding his two sons, Ḥasan and Ḥusayn, and their mother, Fāṭima."

"By God, that is great honour," declared al-Ḥajjāj.[14]

So great was this propaganda and this bribing of people with money, gifts, positions and forcing the nobles to marry their daughters to men who were beneath them in nobility and lineage — which was a practice outside the customs and traditions of the Arabs — that they made men compete to hate a man when they knew nothing of his great merit and position. He had done nothing to merit such hatred and enmity which they brought against him and his descendants.

Those who sought prizes and rewards because of their hostile attacks on him and his descendants were many. Yet how many were those among them who were in reality not ignorant of the true position of ᶜAlī and his descendants in this world and the next? Yet such persons treated them as enemies out of desire for rewards and in expectation of the gifts and bounties which the enemies of ᶜAlī would shower on them. Among such examples is that the killer of al-Ḥusayn b. ᶜAlī b. Abī Ṭālib came to Yazīd b. Muᶜāwiya with the prisoners of al-Ḥusayn's family and addressed him with the following words:

> Fill my saddle bag with silver and gold, for I have killed the concealed king.
> I have killed the man with the best mother and father of all the people and the best of them in lineage — when men trace their lineage.[15]

When Abū Hurayra came to Iraq with Muᶜāwiya in the year of unity, he went to the mosque of Kūfa. When he saw the great number of people who received him, he fell to his knees, struck his bald head several times and said: "People of Iraq, do you allege that I tell lies about God and His Apostle and that my soul will burn in hell-fire. By God I have heard the Apostle of God, may God bless him and his family, say: 'Every prophet has his sanctuary and my sanctuary in Medina is the area between the mountain ᶜĪr and the mountain Thawr, whoever commits an offence in it, the curse of God, of the angels and of all the people will be on him. I testify before God that ᶜAlī committed an offence in it.' "

When Muᶜāwiya was informed of these words of his, he approved of him and was generous to him; he appointed him governor of Medina.[16]

This matter reached such a point with the people that they no longer spoke the truth. Through the power of the enemies of ᶜAlī and the enemies of his righteous descendants they forgot, or at least some of them pretended to forget, about ᶜAlī and his descendants. Thus, when anything good happened in this connection, even some just men greeted it with perplexity and amazement. When ᶜUmar b. ᶜAbd al-ᶜAzīz, the Umayyad Caliph, forbade the cursing of ᶜAlī, some of the towns continued the practice of cursing him out of fear that the report of its prohibition was not true. When ᶜUmar b. ᶜAbd al-ᶜAzīz wrote to his financial agent in Medina ordering him to share out ten thousand dīnārs among the descendants of ᶜAlī b. Abī Ṭālib, this financial agent hesitated as if he had heard an order which could not have been issued. Then as if it was his duty to check it before carrying it out he wrote to ᶜUmar b. ᶜAbd al-ᶜAzīz, saying: "ᶜAlī has descendants in several clans of Quraysh. Among which of his descendants shall I divide up this sum?"

ᶜUmar b. ᶜAbd al-ᶜAzīz wrote back to him: "If I wrote to you about slaughtering a sheep, would you write back about whether it should be black or white?"[17]

VIII

Among the means of propaganda used against ᶜAlī and his Shīᶜa was the fable of ᶜAbd Allāh b. Saba'. This imaginary personality never existed at all. He was invented by Sayf b. ᶜUmar al-Tamīmī, who died in the time of Ḥārūn al-Rashīd, some time after 170 A.H. His ignoble purpose in doing this was hidden from the majority of historians. They imagined – without any proper investigation and examination – that it was true and impossible to disprove. Sayf b. ᶜUmar reported through his forged authorities that ᶜAbd Allāh b. Saba' was a Jew who became a Muslim during the reign of ᶜUthmān. He began to interpolate Jewish stories and other reports whose purpose was to shake the Islamic creed through what these reports attributed to ᶜAlī and the lies which opposed its essence and inner meaning. According to Sayf b. ᶜUmar, the Shīᶜa of ᶜAlī believed them and adopted them as basic principles. The revelation of this interpolation aimed by ᶜAbd Allāh b. Saba' against Islam escaped the Shīᶜa.

It is clear that this fable which Sayf b. ᶜUmar forged with his fabricated authorities did not find any support at the time until, nearly a century and a half after the death of Sayf b. ᶜUmar, al-Ṭabarī came along. He reported it in his book for the first time. From then it began to be regarded as if it were a true story about a true person. Then it took a long time when the idea came among the people that the story of ᶜAbd Allāh b. Saba' was one of the ways to show hatred of ᶜAlī, his descendants and his Shīᶜa, and Sayf b. ᶜUmar had invented it for the purposes of slander and propaganda. Some found a justification for approving of it after Ibn Jarīr al-Ṭabarī had reported it and accepted an evidence which was of defamatory nature. He had cloaked it with the cloak of true proof and attributed to it the name of Jewish stories and had stuck it on the followers of ᶜAlī and his Shīᶜa. Yet it had not occurred to anyone to notice that between the existence of ᶜAbd Allāh

b. Saba' – if he really existed – and the existence of Sayf b. ᶜUmar who created that imaginary personality there was approximately a century and a half. During that long period of time there had lived many narrators and historians. So why did not one of them report this account before Sayf b. ᶜUmar and give support to the existence of ᶜAbd Allāh b. Saba'?

The distance in time between Sayf b. ᶜUmar and Ibn Jarīr al-Ṭabarī is also about a century and a half. So why didn't historians and traditionists report this story of ᶜAbd Allāh b. Saba' before al-Ṭabarī?

No one has asked why these forgeries and lies which are named Jewish stories were intended to be directed against ᶜAlī and his Shīᶜa and why such stories were reported by him and attributed to him when at first sight they seem to be the kinds of thing which raise the esteem of ᶜAlī (especially among the ignorant and those who are not familiar with the Islamic understanding, Islamic law and its philosophy). However, in the deeper sense, they diminish the estimation of ᶜAlī, stir up hatred against him, remove true knowledge of him and obscure him with fanciful ideas so that the eyes are prevented from truly seeing him. Thus when the faulty vision of these fanciful ideas has eliminated true knowledge, there does not remain in the personality of ᶜAlī anything pleasing or splendid to those who only see through that faulty vision. Therefore, the scope for denigrating his greatness and the faith of his Shīᶜa in him becomes wide and easy for his opponents.[18]

Since we have examined the reality of Sayf b. ᶜUmar al-Asadī al-Tamīmī in some detail, it is easy for us to know how to recognise his true nature from what we read in his books and to conclude that his sympathies for the Umayyads led him on several occasions to fabricate and forge accounts as one of the kinds of propaganda exercised for the Umayyads by means of forged religious accounts, traditions and events.

Men such as Sayf b. ᶜUmar are many, whether in the early Islamic era or later. They were those who forged accounts and narrations and told lies against God, His Apostle, the saints and history itself with the intention of belittling the nobility of ᶜAlī and his descendants. Among them were not a few of the great scholars of religious science, literature and history . . . !!

Thus Abū Ḥayyān al-Tawḥīdī, one of the scholars of language and men of letters in the fourth century A. H., did not allow his knowledge and his literary ability to intervene between himself and his hatred of ᶜAlī. Nor did the passing of more than three and half centuries between himself and the death of ᶜAlī stop him from acquainting us with those disgraceful accounts which he fabricated and which he falsely attributed to the Caliph Abū Bakr, to ᶜUmar b. al-Khaṭṭāb and to ᶜAlī b. Abī Ṭālib. Those fabricated accounts were crammed with disparagement of ᶜAlī and with contempt for his situation. A number of historians have accepted them as models because of the literary ability of Abū Ḥayyān to invent such stylish lies and to present them in such an exquisite form.

Yet other historians have rebutted these fabrications and declared them to be lies from the very first day in which they were spread by Abū Ḥayyān al-Tawḥīdī. Even Abū Ḥayyān, himself, has admitted his invention of such lies and false attribution of them to the Caliphs when someone accused him of it. He said that he had been compelled to do that out of annoyance with one of those who loved ᶜAlī and his Shīᶜa. This man used to attend the gathering which Abū Ḥayyān used to visit. ᶜAli's name was never mentioned in this gathering without this sympathiser with the Shīᶜa of ᶜAlī speaking at length about the great qualities of ᶜAlī, beginning by reporting traditions on his authority and going on to give an account of his outstanding merits.[19]

Abū Ḥayyān describes what his motive was: "I wanted to humiliate this man. So I invented this fabrication in order to stop him from enjoying speaking of ᶜAlī and his virtues."[20]

The passing of many centuries after the death of ᶜAlī should have been enough to make the enemy of ᶜAlī forget his enmity, the envious forget his envy and the one who sought blood vengeance forget that desire for blood vengeance. However, as has been explained, not even the passing of time, not even culture and knowledge, were able to change what was in their hearts.

Such were the means and techniques of propaganda and awakening desire, which were in hands of strong, clever and violent enemies who were given the power which they were given. Yet they were unable to root out the name of the person from existence. Indeed they were only able to consolidate his position through providing one hostile version amid many other versions. For the greatness of ᶜAlī was like the sun, he existed in the same way and, in the same way, it will continue. Even though mists, clouds and dust hide it for a time, it still rises. In the final analysis, no barriers, however great, are capable of hiding it from the eyes and thoughts and minds of men.

The awakening of desire by the totality of its means and propaganda with all its different techniques were not the only weapons which were drawn against ᶜAlī, his descendants and his Shīᶜa and followers. Yet even more harm came to ᶜAlī and his righteous descendants as a result of the weapon of intimidation than the harm which came to them as a result of the weapon of awakening desire. Yet the greatness of ᶜAlī, for which history has no parallel after the greatness of the Prophet, has challenged the techniques of intimidation, just as it challenged the techniques of awakening desire, in a miraculous way whose like history has never seen.

IX

Intimidation

Al-Masᶜūdī reports: In the year 53 A.H. Muᶜāwiya b. Abī Sufyān killed Ḥujr b. ᶜAdī. He was the first to be killed in captivity in Islam with no guilt levelled against him. This Ḥujr was one of the close adherents of ᶜAlī b. Abī Ṭālib and one of those who was against ᶜAlī's cursing from public pulpits. Ziyād had him sent from Kūfa together with nine of his companions from the inhabitants of Kūfa and four others. Muᶜāwiya sent a man to them, who met them on the road. He said to Ḥujr: "The Commander of the faithful" – he means Muᶜāwiya – "has commanded me to kill you and to kill your companions, you the leader of error, the source of unbelief and tyranny, you follower of Abū Turāb (i.e. ᶜAlī); unless you withdraw from your unbelief, curse your leader and renounce him."

Some did that and renounced ᶜAlī out of fear. However, Ḥujr and his group of the men would not do that. Ḥujr said: "Steadfastness in the face of the blade of your sword is easier for us than what you demand us to do. Going to God, and to His Prophet and to his heir and trustee is preferable to us than entering Hell."

Then Ḥujr was slaughtered just like sheep are slaughtered. Those of his companions who agreed with his words, followed him to death. Who is there who sees or hears of such martyrdom and does not feel terror and fear at the oppression against them from the enemies of ᶜAlī and of his descendants?

One of the dreadful acts of intimidation and persecution which occurred was when Muᶜāwiya b. Abī Sufyān sent Busr b. Arṭa'a –

who was a man who went beyond even the limits of cruelty, mercilessness and dishonour – to Ḥijāz and Yemen to root out all those who loved ᶜAlī b. Abī Ṭālib. He ordered him to wipe them out without any mercy or compassion. The following passage occurs in Ibn Abī al-Ḥadīd's commentary on *Nahj al-Balāgha*:

"Muᶜawiya sent Busr b. Arṭa'a to Yemen with a large army. He ordered him to kill everyone who acknowledged obedience to ᶜAlī, peace be on him. He killed a great number of people including the two sons of ᶜUbayd Allāh b. ᶜAbbās b. ᶜAbd al-Muṭṭalib."[21]

It is well-known in history that the two sons of ᶜUbayd Allāh b. ᶜAbbās were just young boys. Busr killed them merely because of their close relationship with ᶜAlī b. Abī Ṭālib. So how do you think it was possible for any one to declare publicly his love for ᶜAlī after that? Or how could he do it when he sees or hears of this general massacre which history describes and then sees or hears of two innocent young boys killed in captivity for no other crime than their relationship with ᶜAlī b. Abī Ṭālib?

George Jirdaq mentions in his book, *Imām ᶜAlī*, that the war-cry of Muᶜāwiya was: "There are soldiers of God in honey". He meant by that the honey which is mixed with poison and then administered to his opponents. It is this same honey with which Muᶜāwiya killed al-Ḥasan b. ᶜAlī. Then he proceeded to buy people with money from the public treasury and thus contrived to create supporters and fighters. When the people showed their displeasure with his son, Yazīd and refused to pledge allegiance to him, he spoke threateningly to them:

"He who gives a warning to men is excused from the consequences of their failure to heed it. I have addressed you in the past and men among you have stood up before me and declared me to be a liar before the people. I swear before God that if anyone of you replies to me with even one word, no other word will come to him before the sword reaches his head. Every man should only look after himself."[22]

X

What man is there who would say anything after this with such a threat ringing in his ears? Who is the one who would be able to raise his voice when he sees and hears the demands of the Umayyads to go out to fight al-Ḥusayn on the plain of Karbalā' and not go? What intimidation available could be used by the enemies of ᶜAlī and the enemies of his descendants, is there greater than the massacre which they brought down on al-Ḥusayn, his children, his followers and his bereft family. Such killing is the kind of cruelty and disgraceful action which history has never seen the life of in all its epochs.

A little before the battle, al-Ḥusayn stood and addressed the army of Yazīd with the following words:

". . . Look back at my lineage and see who I am. Then examine yourselves and reprove their proceedings. Examine whether it is good and lawful for you to kill me and to violate my womenfolk. Am I not the son of the daughter of your Prophet and the son of his trustee, his cousin? Is not Ja^cfar, the martyr, who flies in heaven, my uncle? Haven't you heard the well-known tradition that the Apostle of God said, to me and my brother: 'You two are the lords of the youth of Paradise and the delight of the eyes of people who observe my practice'? If you believe what I say – and what I say is the truth, for by God I have never told a lie since I learnt that God hated those who lie (there the point is proved). But if you do not believe me, there are among you those who will tell you about that if you ask them. Ask Jābir b. ʿAbd Allāh, or Abū Saʿīd al-Khudrī or Sahl b. Saʿd or Zayd b. Arqam. They will tell you that they heard the Apostle of God say that. In those words there is a barrier which should prevent you from shedding my blood."

Al-Ḥusayn went on with his speech and said:

"Tell me do you want me killed to avenge the death of one of you whom I have killed? Or because of property belonging to you which I have expropriated? Or to avenge some wound which I have inflicted upon you?"

The people's answer to that question was the onslaught by which they blackened the face of history and which drew them on to strike the neck of al-Ḥusayn and the necks of his sons and helpers with their swords. That day did not end until seventy-two corpses had fallen. Their heads were cut off and their bodies trampled by horses. Then a shout arose: "Burn down the tents of the wrongdoers". Then fire began to devour the tents of al-Ḥusayn and his followers. The women and children fled in terror, not knowing with whom they might seek refuge and with whom they might find a shelter. The bereft family of al-Ḥusayn was led away captive. They were marched around the towns and villages. The head of al-Ḥusayn and the heads of his sons and followers were held aloft on spears in the sight of the captives of the family of the Apostle of God.

When they brought the head of al-Ḥusayn before Yazid b. Muᶜāwiya in Syria, they put it on a tray. Yazid began to poke at the teeth in it with a cane and he recited:

> We have cut off heads of men who were dear to us but they were too refractory and wrong.[23]

Who is there who could see these sights or hear of such a massacre, of such maltreatment, of such an appalling act against the family of ᶜAli and not be seized with fear and dismay? Then how could the name of ᶜAlī continue to shine forth while this was some of what was waged against him and what was waged against his descendants with those murderous weapons unless ᶜAlī was unique and unless he was the only model among men in the world?

Muslim b. ᶜUqba, one of the protegés of Yazid b. Muᶜāwiya: (and he who was created with a venomous nature, a man in snakeskin, to use the definition of the Egyptian writer al-ᶜAqqād) this man reached the ultimate in persecution of the followers of ᶜAlī and the followers of al-Ḥusayn. He was, in the description of the historian, one-eyed and ruddy-faced with an agitated head. When he walked, it was as if he was pulling his legs out of mud.

He attained such a degree of voracity for evil that even when he was a very old and sick man, he allowed Medina, the sanctuary of the Prophet, peace be on him, to be sacked. He allowed it to be sacked fo. three days. He massacred its inhabitants by the sword in the same way as butchers slaughter sheep so that feet sank into the blood. He killed the sons of the Emigrants and the Anṣār and the offspring of men who had fought at Badr. He made all the Companions and the following generations of Muslims, whom he had spared, pledge allegiance to Yazīd b. Muᶜāwiya on the basis of being a slave of the Commander of the faithful (i.e. of Yazīd).

He sent his army into the area around the grave of the Prophet seizing people, property and violating women . . . until the dead reached the total, in the estimation of al-Zuhrī, of seven hundred of the leaders of the people and ten thousand of their retainers. Then he wrote to Yazīd describing what he had done as if he was describing a jubilant conquering hero. After a lengthy description, he wrote:

"We sent the cavalry against them... I did not pray the noon prayer except in their mosque after a devastating battle and great plunder. (Thus he writes). We had plunged our swords into them. We killed those of them who advanced towards us and we pursued those who fled. We put their wounded to death. (Thus he writes). We plundered the city for three days as ordered by the Commander of the faithful (Yazīd), may God fortify support of him. I had the houses of the children of the martyr, ᶜUthmān b. ᶜAffān, put under protection and security. Praise be to God who has cured my breast by enabling me to fight against men who have long been in dispute and have been great in hypocrisy, how often have they been recalcitrant, how long have they been tyrannical.

"I write this letter to the Commander of the faithful while I am sick and weak in the house of Saᶜīd b. al-ᶜĀs. I only see myself returning to God. I do not care when I die after having taken part in this battle".[24]

XI

Al-ᶜAqqād says in his analysis of this hatred: "This blazing hatred within this rotten mind was only the hatred found in the characters of deformed and distorted men which could make him imagine that it was a hatred borne out of a desire to avenge the death of ᶜUthmān or against revolt by the people against the kingdom of Yazīd."

The hatred was aimed against ᶜAlī b. Abī Ṭālib and his descendants and supporters. Many of them became victims of that cruelty and greed in the Ḥijāz, in Yemen or in Iraq, where ᶜAlī, his descendants and supporters were most violently repressed.

When Zayd b. ᶜAlī b. al-Ḥusayn was killed in Kūfa, his followers were afraid of him being dismembered – just as the family of ᶜAlī were too afraid of the dismemberment of Imam ᶜAlī's body by his enemies to bury his body publicly or make a tomb at his grave. So when it was night and when the people were still not aware that Zayd b. ᶜAlī b. al-Ḥusayn had been killed, they buried him at the river Yaᶜqūb. They dammed the river and dug a grave for him in its bed. Then they buried him in his clothes and let the water flow back over it. However, informers gave the secret away and his Umayyad enemies took his body out. They cut off his head and nailed his body to a cross and had guards set over it so that it could not be taken down. The body remained guarded for a long time. His head was sent to Hishām b. ᶜAbd al-Mālik and he ordered it to be set up on the gate into Damascus. Then he sent it to Medina and then it was taken to Egypt and set up in the mosque there until some Egyptians stole it and buried it.[25]

When al-Walīd succeeded to authority, he wrote to his governor in

Iraq, Yusuf b. ʿUmar al-Thaqafī, saying to him: "When this letter of mine comes to you, look for the calf of Iraq (meaning the body of Zayd b. ʿAlī) and burn it and scatter the ashes into the Sea".

Yūsuf b. ʿUmar carried out his command and he ordered Kharrāsh b. Hawshab: "Take Zayd's body down from his cross and set fire to it. Then break up the bits and put them in a date-basket. Take them on a boat and scatter them in the Euphrates."[26]

Is there any event reported in history more abominable, crueler and more terrible than the foul crimes which the enemies of ʿAli and his descendants committed against ʿAlī and his descendants? Surely those who are set aside by history for different kinds of torture and for notorious crimes are none other than those who were enemies of ʿAlī and his descendants? If the grave of Imam ʿAlī had been known at first, would they have ever disregarded it and kept away from desecrating it?

XII

Hishām wrote to his governor in Baṣra, al-Qāsim b. Muḥammad al-Thaqafī, to move all the Hāshimites in Iraq to Medina because of the fear that they might rebel. Similarly he wrote to his governor in Medina to detain some of them, to inspect them once every week and to get guarantors on their behalf that they would not leave there. Al-Fadl b. ʿAbd al-Raḥmān has given us a picture of their treatment, articulating their sentiments, in a long poem. Some of this we present here as a fleeting glimpse into some of this cruel treatment which the ʿAlids met at the hands of their enemies. The full version is presented by Ibn Abi al-Ḥadīd in *Sharḥ Nahj al-Balāgha*:

Whenever they cause any discontent in any
 land, they put us into prisons or expel us.
My God, feared by all, may not suffice those who
 have taken us to Medina as prisoners.
They kill us without any crime being done against
 them. May God be the One who fights against
 a people who kill us.
They make us the closest of enemies of theirs
 and they swim in our blood.
Where are our dead whom you have unjustly treated
 and wrongfully killed?

Bring back Hāshim and return Abū al-Yaqẓān
and Ibn Budayl among others.
Bring back the man of two testimonies and the
dead in fighting against whom you were
wickedly involved.
Then return Ḥujr and the companions of Ḥujr in
whose killing you once unjustly took part.
Then return Abū ᶜUmayr and return Rushayd and
Maytham and those
Of the Hashimites who were killed on the banks
of the river at the battle with Ḥusayn.
And return Ḥusayn.

Al-Faḍl goes on in his poem to include with these, those killed at Karbalā', Muslim b. ᶜAqīl, Zayd b. ᶜAlī and others.

The ᶜAlids disdain the idea of gaining vengeance from their opponents whenever they gained victory over them. They have followed in the footsteps of their ancestor ᶜAlī b. Abī Ṭālib in magnanimity, forgiveness and forbearance toward those who curse, persecute and fight them, all things by which ᶜAlī was distinguished. That was one of the eternal natural qualities of which he had become a symbol and to which the secret of ᶜAlī's constancy in time belongs.

I have read – and I do not remember where – that one of the Umayyad Caliphs – it was probably ᶜUmar b. ᶜAbd al-ᶜAzīz – had learnt that Hishām b. Ismāᶜil, an Umayyad governor of the Ḥijāz, was creating excuses to injure the family of the house of the Prophet, and especially ᶜAlī b. al-Ḥusayn. The Caliph dismissed him and ordered that he stand outside so that those who had a complaint against him could go past and register it. Imam ᶜAlī b. al-Ḥusayn was summoned. He was the person of the family of the Prophet who had received the worst oppression and persecution from this governor. It was demanded of him that he go past the man and recount the harm which he had suffered from him. So he went past in accordance with the insistence of the Caliph's orders. However, he went past this cruel wicked Hishām b. Ismāᶜīl and looked at him but he did not say a word of complaint and he did not mention his wrongdoing. He did not even indicate, not with slightest indication, what this governor had done to him and the family of the Apostle. When Imam ᶜAlī b. al-Ḥusayn had withdrawn from him and the governor was still standing abject and humiliated, the latter called out, seeing his unwillingness to do him harm and his avoidance of denouncing him, he called out at the top of his voice: "God knows best where to entrust His Message."

Among the best to describe the behaviour of the ᶜAlids and the images of their natural dispositions was the poet, Diᶜbil al-Khuzāᶜī, who says of them;

Have you not seen that for thirty years I have
 come and gone with constant sighs?
I see their wealth divided among others while
 their own hands have become empty of wealth.
When they are wronged against, they stretch out to the
 authors of their harassment hands which shrink
 away from vengeance.
The daughters of Ziyād are protected in palaces
 while the daughter of the Apostle of God is
 in the wilderness.

Thus, when they were mistreated, they would stretch out towards those who mistreated them hands which knew nothing of hatred and vengeance.

XIII

Al-Mansur treated the ᶜAlids the way he did and history has reported the violence of al-Manṣūr against the descendants of ᶜAlī b. Abī Ṭālib in a way which makes bodies tremble at the bloodshed, murderous blows and the different kinds of imprisonment in dungeons and the belly of the earth, where these were imprisoned. Muḥammad ᶜAlī al-Ẓāhir says: "Al-Manṣūr used to imprison the political suspects of the family of the Prophet in dungeons. He would chain them in iron fetters, beat them, break their limbs, flog them and gouge out their eyes. They could not see light, nor day, nor night. Indeed they would know the passing of time by their recitation of portions of the Qur'ān. From time to time a call would come among these prisoners: "Choose one from among you for us to kill". Then they would vie with each other for death (see al-Ṭabarī's History).[27]

Al-Manṣūr especially treated the descendants of al-Ḥasan b. ᶜAlī with the most cruel treatment which an angry wild beast might use. However, there are limits to the anger and cruelty of an angry wild beast. As for al-Manṣūr, history was not aware of any limits to his bestiality until he died. He seized from the family of ᶜAlī, their revered old leaders, like ᶜAbd Allāh al-Maḥḍ b. al-Ḥasan b. ᶜAlī b. Abī Ṭālib, who was the leader of the clan descended from Abū Ṭālib at that time. Al-Manṣūr seized his son, his brothers and his nephews, who were the leaders of the descendants of al-Ḥasan and he imprisoned them. He killed a number of them in prison and the others died there.[28] It is reported that the chamberlain of al-Manṣūr once went out and said: "Let whoever of the descendants of al-Ḥasan is at the door come in." The revered old men of the descendants of al-Ḥasan entered. He took them into a side room and then brought in blacksmiths from another door. He had them chained and taken to prison. He kept them in prison in Kūfa until they died there.

One of the strange examples of the oppression of al-Manṣūr is the story that one of the ᶜAlids came and stood before al-Manṣūr.

"What brings you?" al-Manṣūr asked him.

"I came so that you could imprison me with my family", he replied "for I do not want to live in the world without them".

So he imprisoned him with them. That man was ᶜAlī b. al-Ḥasan b. al-Ḥasan b. ᶜAlī b. Abī Ṭālib. He was one of the most handsome men and used to be called "Yellow Silk" because of his handsomeness. Al-Manṣūr had him brought before him and said:

"Are you Yellow Silk?"

"This is what people say", he replied.

"Then let me kill you in a way I have never killed anyone" said al-Manṣūr.

He ordered a pillar to be built over him while he was alive and then he died in it.[29]

This is all in addition to al-Mansūr's pursuit and murder of Nafs al-Zakiyya and his pursuit of Ibrāhīm b. ᶜAbd Allāh and the hundreds of famous leaders of the ᶜAlids whom the ᶜAbbāsids pursued and drove into distant lands. Many of them were compelled to hide in remote villages and among far off tribes, to change their names, their clothes and their appearances, to gather among Christian communities and to pretend to hold religious beliefs which were not their true belief. Some involved themselves so deeply in their hiding that a time came when the sons of those men in hiding only knew a little about their family. Among these few ᶜAlids – as I know – is the great Lebanese poet, Amīn Nakhla, in Beirut. Among them is the distinguished man of letters, Badīᶜ Hāshim Bikfir Shīmā. As for those whom the expulsion caused to lose the memory of their ancestors, it is not unlikely that they may go beyond tens in terms of the principal ancestors and hundreds and thousands in terms of their descendants.

XIV

George Jirdaq alludes to the verses of Abū al-ᶜAlā' al-Maᶜarrī concerning ᶜAlī and al-Ḥusayn, when al-Maᶜarrī says:

On the surface of time
There are two witnesses of the shedding of the blood
of the two martyrs, ᶜAlī and his son.
They appear in the beginning of the night
as the two twilights.
And at the end of it as the two dawns.
These have remained
clung to the shirt of time to arrive
at the Day of Judgement
ready to bear witness in the presence of the Merciful!

Jirdaq says: "I see from the agony of emotion in these three lines and the revolution of thought and feeling behind them, that it is appropriate to apply these passionate exciting words, within the compass of the ᶜAlid tragedy, to the sufferings of the supporters of right, who were harmed, whipped, persecuted, driven into the wilderness to die of hunger and cold, buried alive, crucified and burnt with their sons and brothers refusing to betray their inner consciences; and renounced Imam ᶜAlī in slave-like fashion. And rejected the nobility of human creation which the Imam represented in his life.

"It strikes me to feel that the ᶜAlid tragedy which stretched over long epochs is revived in these three verses both in substance and spirit."[30]

Al-Sayyid Aḥmad Ṣaqr who undertook the commentary and edition of the book *The Martyrdoms of the Family of Abū Ṭālib* (*Maqātil al-Ṭālibiyyīn*) by Abū al-Faraj al-Isfahānī says in his introduction: "History has not known a family like the family of Abū Ṭālib, which, having attained the zenith of nobility and perfection in its origin, has had its rights taken from it." He goes on to say: "The opponents of this pure family have exceeded all bounds by making war against it. They have made it suffer the blows of violent mistreatment and imposed all kinds of torture on it. They have treated it ruthlessly, respecting neither its right nor its sanctity. They have poured down great wrong on all its womenfolk, children and men with a violence untouched by gentleness and with cruelty undiluted by compassion so that the tragedies of the family have become proverbial for dreadful mistreatment. Yet this excessive cruelty has awoken the springs of mercy and love in the hearts of people, spread forth the sorrow which was implicit in their consciences and filled their entire spirits with grief. The deaths of these martyrs have become accounts which are recounted, reports which are handed down and stories in which people find satisfaction for their emotions and relief for their feelings. So they have eagerly searched for them.

"Reporters of historical tradition and writers have sought to answer the call of this strong desire which is the search for the personification of perfection among people. So they began to compile reports about them, to set out their great virtues, to write about their lives and to record their martyrdoms.

"Among these scholars was Abū Mikhnaf who died in 170 A.H. (785/6). He wrote *The Martyrdom of ᶜAlī (Maqtal ᶜAlī)*[31] and *The Martyrdom of al-Ḥusayn (Maqtal al-Ḥusayn).*[32]

"Others included:

Naṣr b. Muzāhim, died in 212 A.H. (826/7), who wrote *The Martyrdom of al-Ḥusayn (Maqtal al-Ḥusayn).*[33]

Al-Haytham b. ᶜAdī, died 208 A.H. (8222/3), who wrote *Reports about al-Ḥasan and his Death (Akhbār al-Ḥasan wa-Wifātihi).*[34]

Al-Wāqidī, who wrote *The Martyrdom of al-Ḥasan (Maqtal al-Ḥasan)* and *The Martyrdom of al-Ḥusayn (Maqtal al-Ḥusayn).*[35]

Ibn al-Naṭṭāḥ, who wrote *The Martyrdom of Zayd b. ᶜAlī (Maqtal Zayd ibn ᶜAlī).*[36].

Al-Ghallābī, who wrote *The Martyrdom of ᶜAlī (Maqtal ᶜAlī)* and *The Martyrdom of al-Ḥusayn (Maqtal al-Ḥusayn).*[37]

Al-Ashnānī, who wrote *The Martyrdom of al-Ḥasan (Maqtal al-Ḥasan)* and *The Martyrdom of Zayd b. ᶜAlī (Maqtal Zayd ibn ᶜAlī).*[38]

Umar b. Shabbah, who wrote *The Martyrdom of Muḥammad and Ibrahim, the two sons of ᶜAbd Allāh b. al-Ḥasan. (Maqtal Muḥammad wa-Ibrāhīm ibnay ᶜAbd Allah ibn al-Ḥasan).*[39]

Al-Madā'inī, died 225 A. H. (838/9) who wrote a book entitled, *The Names of the Members of the Family of Abū Ṭālib who have been killed (Asmā man qatala min al-Ṭālibiyyin).*[40]

"Then came Abū al-Faraj al-Isfahānī, who died in 356 A. H. (967). He composed *The Martyrdom of the Members of the Family of Abū Ṭālib (Maqātil al-Ṭālibiyyīn* or the name Ibn Nadīm gives it *Maqātil Āl Abī Ṭālib).*[41] In it he describes the lives of the martyrs of the descendants of Abū Ṭālib from the period of the Apostle to the time in which he began to write his book, which was in the month of Jamādā al-Awwal, 313 A.H. (924/5).

"Up to that time, Abū al-Faraj had described more than two

hundred martyrs from the Family of Abū Ṭālib. All of them were the very summit of men, Imams and leaders, great men of literature, of poetry, of knowledge and of virtue, who were killed wrongfully and by aggression by the swords of those who were full of hatred and enmity towards them and ᶜAlī."[42]

XV

There are hundreds of examples of the attempts at propaganda on the one hand and violence on the other towards ᶜAlī and his descendants in order to wipe out their roots, which the reader will find in all the books which were written in earlier times. There are hundreds of examples also in the modern books which have been written about ᶜAlī and his descendants and the sufferings and persecution which they received from their enemies, like the book of ᶜAbd al-Fattāḥ Maqsūd, the book of Shaykh ᶜAbd Allāh al-ᶜAlāyilī, the book of George Jirdaq, the book of ᶜAbbās al-Aqqād, the book of Shaykh Maḥmūd (Abū Riyya), the book of Jurji Zaydān, the book of Shaykh Khālid Muḥammad Khālid and many others. There are hundreds of books written in foreign languages which demonstrate the bad treatment and persecution directed against ᶜAlī and his family. These are all in addition to the immense number of different kinds of wicked acts committed against them which are mentioned as examples in the expositions of works of biography, prose and poetry. These include the incredible actions which the opponents of ᶜAlī used in order to wipe out his memory, to remove any trace of him, to lead men's thoughts astray and to distort his true nature. It is not unlikely that the memory of him which history has lost through the techniques which the opponents of ᶜAlī adopted to wipe out and remove his name, is very great, though its corroboration is not possible for historians. Or else its memory may have been neglected deliberately, especially in poetry against him, out of respect for ᶜAlī's position because of the repugnant curses which it contained.

Despite all this, ᶜAlī has remained, as he still does, the purest of all souls after the Apostle of God, a man in whom all human qualities are represented so that they keep him for as long as time remains as an example of noble-mindedness, integrity, compassion, sympathy, justice and literature, the like of which was not known after the literature of the noble Qur'ān. He is an example of gigantic intellect whose descriptive powers baffled earlier generations and which is still the source of amazement even in more recent times. This personality will continue to be the subject of study by scholars in the fields of wisdom, philosophy and literature for as long as God wishes and to the end of the life of mankind, if there is an end to the life of mankind. All this will be so because of the multiplicity of the factors and aspects of that intellect and the extent of the horizons it encompasses.

Whenever history is negligent – and it is seldom negligent despite the factors of intimidation and inducement – and fails to remember the name of ᶜAlī, there arise scores of his sons in different roles to remind people of ᶜAlī and his great value. By their merits and values in the life of mankind and in human existence through the life which they present to the people, the people's hearts are captivated and examples are given to the highest extent of praise which man can attain. Then tongues constantly repeat the name of ᶜAlī and his great merits are praised.

ᶜAbbās Maḥmūd al-ᶜAqqād says: "... you go down the generations of descendants of the family of Abū Ṭālib, the sons of ᶜAlī and Fāṭima the fair, for a hundred years, two hundred years and four hundred years, then one of their men stands out before you and it appears to you that this long time has not separated the branch from the root in great qualities and practices. It is as if he came after a few days not after hundreds and hundreds of years. You cannot wait to cry out: These are ᶜAlī's qualities. There is no doubt about that. For you hear this man from among them talking and replying to those who talk to him. You see him working and being competent in his work. There is no mistake in his conversation, nor in his work. There is no mistaking that eloquence and clarity, nor that intelligence and that statement which brings silence, nor those characteristics by which the fame of ᶜAlī and his family has been spread far and wide. You can unite them all in two words which point most faithfully to them: The perfection of chivalry.

"It is a pure character, an eloquent tongue, a steadfastness which completely embraces man and morals, a pride which does not pay attention to benefits which may escape it when it has set out along the path of manhood and the path of its ancestors."[43]

This personality – the personality of Imam ᶜAlī – which has defied time and defied every actual measure, some of whose effect was capable of changing the reality and situation of nations and the reality of the course of history... this personality filled, and still does, the eyes and hearts of men with love and admiration. It was an ideal model for men of intelligence and discernment concerned with perfect humanity in the world of men. This personality could not be fettered because it stood firm and resolute like a mountain before the hurricanes and storms, the thunder and lightning, which were weaved around it by every shape and kind of propaganda including promises and threats, bribery and violence. It has become the cause of life and the centre of hope despite all the wars which have been waged over it. To such an extent is this the case that books have been written about it, studies made of it and quotations and proverbs made from it. It is a lamp which guides those lost amid the oppressions of the world. Researchers aim at its reality, become involved in the traces and become immersed in it. They come from East and West, Arab and non-Arab, Muslim and non-Muslim. Not a day goes by without a new book appearing from scholars, men of letters, philosophers and historians, which convey a new idea about this wonderful, extra-ordinary personality which has coined the most wonderful phrases for the loftiest of thought in the greatest of spirits from the world of man. Time cannot disturb or change anything of its essence.

This book, whose preface I am writing at the insistent request of its author, and of the one who generously financed its publication and of its publisher, is one of those books which authors bring before us from time to time which illuminates a new aspect and a new idea about the unique personality of Imam ᶜAlī.

When I say that he requested me to write the preface with great insistence in the face of my refusal and clear apology, I do not say that out of conceit and pride. I only say it because of my knowledge of my own inadequacy – and I say this with certainty – to undertake to write a word that would be appropriate as introduction to a book which is devoted to the personality of this unique Imam who will live as long as time goes on. Although I was compelled to accede to their wish, I am still sure that I am unworthy of such a task as this.

The idea of this book arose first in the mind of the eminent merchant, al-Sayyid Hāshim Shubar, when he realised that there were writers who can write down ideas about Imam ᶜAlī and compile new books on new aspects of the life of the Commander of the faithful. He contributed the means and the expenses, which he divided between them and the costs of printing their books. Among these books was a substantial collection written by the well-known preacher al-Ustādh Jawād Shubar, one of the first class preachers at commemorative services for al-Ḥusayn.

The merchant, al-Sayyid Hāshim Shubar, is from a deeply learned family. More than one of this family have been in a position of high religious responsibility, in earlier times men like al-Ḥujja ʿAbd Allāh Shubar and in more recent times great scholars like al-Sayyid ʿAlī Shubar in Kuwait and al-Sayyid ʿAbbās Shubar, who combined the spiritual and literary leadership in Baṣra.

Al-Sayyid Hāshim Shubar is a descendant of Hāshim and of ʿAlī. This pedigree binds him to ʿAlī, to devotion to his life and to faith in his principles. He gave the preacher Jawād Shubar the sum of one thousand dinars as a reward for writing the book we have just mentioned. He also made known his readiness to pay all the expenses necessary for the book to be printed and published in a suitable manner.

The preacher, Jawād Shubar, is himself a branch of the Shubar family tree, the family whose great qualities I have already alluded to and some of whose members are well-known for preferring the good of their soul to anything else in many situations. Therefore it was no surprise that he should refuse to accept the gift for himself as a result of that preference. He went on to indicate to al-Sayyid Hāshim that he should set up with that sum of money which he had specified, a competition to write about the personality of Imam ʿAlī on the proviso that the preacher Jawād Shubar would exclude himself from entering the competition.

This idea was welcomed by al-Sayyid Hāshim Shubar and a committee of scholars was formed to examine the works of the contestants in the competition. This book won first prize.

The author of this book is al-Ustādh Sulaymān Kattānī from Biskintā in Lebanon. He is one of the Christian men of letters there. There is no doubt that he is fashioned from that substance which the nature of men causes to derive benefit from its entire existence. Such a nature delights in accounts of glorious deeds, in stories of heroism, in the power of the spirit and devotion to truth. Such a substance, which is formed from this nature, will not settle. It is constantly searching for and continuously enquiring about such qualities among leaders, rulers, philosophers and men of letters. When it comes upon the object of its desire, either wholly or partly, it holds on to it with all the absorption and fascination which exists in it. Then it is influenced by it spiritually and it becomes one of the instruments for spreading it intellectually to the extent that its impact, its understanding and beliefs in it, permits it.

There are many features which support my view of the substance and nature of the author of this book and his love for the form to which good men of good spirits are attracted. When you add to this his literary ability, which has evoked a love of literature in him and has led him to go deeply into books in search of that desire, it is easy for us to understand the secret of Sulaymān Kattāni's love of Imam ᶜAlī, his study of his history and the influence of Imam ᶜAlī's life on him both in his reading and in his writing. It is also easy for us to discern this spirit and this literary ability from these shining pages which the skill of the writer has stylistically set down. I am saying no more than the truth when I say that it is unique. The author has been concerned to record his impressions and to convey his ideas. What he has set out of the life of Imam ᶜAlī is taken from what those who love him have said, from what those who hate him have said, from what those who have neither hatred or love towards him have said, from what the Imam himself has said and what he left for the people to say about him and what they really wanted to say when they went back to their consciences and took wisdom from them.

With this spirit, with this nature and with the impetus of a living conscience, Sulayman Kattānī has written this book of his. In it he has given a picture of the thoughts of a man of letters whom Imam ᶜAlī has attracted by those aspects which the reader will come across and at which the reader will pause for a long time in great amazement.

Jaᶜfar al-Khalīlī — ***Baghdad***

FOOTNOTES TO FOREWORD

1. Al-Mubarrad *al-Kāmil* (Cairo) vol. III, p. 49
2. Al-Masᶜūdī *Murūj al-Dhahab* (Cairo) vol. II, p. 72.
3. ᶜAbd al-Latīf Ḥamza, *al-Madkhal fī Fann al-Taḥrīr al-Ṣuḥufī*, p. 240.
4. *Al-Madkhal fī Mawsūᶜāt al-Atabat al-Muqaddasa*. p. 248
5. *Ibid.* p. 393
6. ᶜAbd al-Laṭīf Ḥamza, *op. cit.*, p. 26.
7. Al-Masᶜūdī, *op. cit.* Vol. II, p. 72.
8. Ibn al-Athīr, *al-Ta'rīkh fī al-Kāmil* (Beirut) Vol. V, p. 42; Ibn al-Ḥadīd, *Sharḥ Nahj al-Balāgha*, Vol. I, p. 357.
9. *Ibid.*
10. *Ibid.*
11. *Ibid.* Vol. I, p. 360.

12. Al-Mubarrad, *op. cit.*, Vol. I, p. 223.
13. Ibn al-Athir *op. cit.*, Vol. IV, p. 585.
14. Ibn Abi al-Ḥadid, *op. cit.*, Vol. I, p. 357.
15. Ibn ᶜAbd Rabbihi, *al-ᶜIqd al-Farid*, Vol. IV, p. 381; al-Masᶜūdi, *Murūj al-Dhahab*, Vol. II, p. 65.
16. Ibn Abi al-Ḥadid, *op. cit.*, Vol. I, p. 359.
17. Al-Masᶜūdi, *op. cit.*, Vol II, p. 168.
18. On the fable of ᶜAbd Allāh b. Saba' see Murtaḍā al-ᶜAskari *ᶜAbd Allāh b. Saba'*.
19. Ibn Abi al-Ḥadid, *op. cit.*, Vol II, pp. 593–597.
20. Ibn Ḥajar al-ᶜAsqalāni, *Lisān al-Mizān*, under *Abū Ḥayyān.*
21. Ibn Abi al-Ḥadid, *op. cit.* Vol. I, p. 113.
22. George Jirdaq, *Imam ᶜAlī*, p. 215.
23. Al-Aqqād, *Abū al-Shuhadā'*, p. 90.
24. *Ibid.*; al-Masᶜūdi, *Murūj al-Dhahab*, Vol. II, p. 65.
25. Al-Zirikli *al-Aᶜlām* (Zayd b. ᶜAlī).
26. Al-Ṭabari, *Ta'rikh al-Umam wa-al-Mulūk* (Cairo) Vol. V, p. 538.
27. Muḥammad ᶜAlī al-Ẓāhir, *Ẓalām al-Sijn*, p. 401.
28. Abu al-Faraj al-Isfahāni, *Maqātil al-Ṭalibiyyin*, p. 178.
29. Ta'rikh al-Duwal al-Islāmiyya, p. 164.
30. *Al-Imām ᶜAlī Sawt al-ᶜAdāla al-Insāniyya*, p. 361. George Jirdaq.
31. Ibn Nadim, *al-Fihrist*, 136.
32. *Ibid.* 137.
33. *Ibid.* 146.
34. *Ibid.*
35. *Ibid.* 144.
36. *Ibid.* 156.
37. *Ibid.* 166.
38. *Ibid.*
39. *Ibid.* 164.
40. *Ibid.*
41. *Muᶜjam al-Udabā'*, p. 148.
42. From the introduction of Abū al-Faraj's *Maqātil al-Ṭalibiyyin* edited and introduction by Aḥmad Ṣaqr.
43. Al-Aqqād *Abū al-Shuhadā'*, p. 51–52.

AUTHOR'S ACKNOWLEDGEMENT

To the judging committee at Najaf through its private secretary, the scholar and preacher, al-Sayyid Jawād Shubar.

I present to your noble committee my book entitled *Imam ʿAlī Source of Light, Wisdom and Might.* At mentioning this great name, I eagerly seek forgiveness for every omission which may have arisen unintentionally on my part, since my pen does not have any greater power to rove around the vast worlds in which the mind of this unique man of genius was able to penetrate. Yet I put forward this effort of mine with the good intention which urges me to such zeal. I have collected by my hand some bunches of flowers to put in this bouquet with the earnest intention that they will facilitate for it some acceptance before this noble presence.

I offer my thanks to your noble committee for granting me the means of putting forward this effort of mine by which I might illuminate myself with the best and most generous man whom the generations of man have known up to the present time.

With all sincerity
Sulaymān Kattānī

Biskintā, Lebanon
1966

DEDICATION

To all who love ʿAlī b. Abī Ṭālib for his heroic values and for opening the windows of the soul to truth, goodness and beauty.

THE OPENING

Opening Remarks

Few are the men who are patterned like ᶜAlī b. Abī Ṭālib . . . Life itself rises with them, as they appear scattered along the crossroads of generations, like lamps. It absorbs the last sparks from them in order to use them as guidance along the ways for the benefit of those who journey. Despite their fewness, they are like pillars through which can be seen the courtyards of temples; holding on their shoulders the heavy weights of the foundation stones, so that the domes of the minaret will flash above their lofty heights.

They are in all that like solid mountains which receive the turbulence of storms and the thunder-clouds so that they can transform them through the purifying filters along their slopes into fine sweet gushing streams of goodness.

These, at every moment of time in the world of man, are the pivots and the pioneers. They are the final end of search and exploration. They are the ultimate destination of every line of thought which penetrates into existence. They are signs towards existence at every crossroad, which prevent the paths to it from going astray. In every wilderness they are laws which prevent those who go astray in it from excess.

In the blackness of night, they are the direction of dawn. And at the sombre grave, they are a source for consolation.

Among these few, the face of ᶜAlī b. Abī Ṭālib emerges in the halo of a prophethood and in the shadow of a mission, which both flow over him in harmony and perfection as he encompasses them in colour and frame.

The opportunity for creation of a man in whom there is a noble abundance of gifts and qualitites, always presents itself when the darkest night prolongs its darkness in any one of the epochs of man in which there has been ignorance, oppresion and injustice which destroy and humiliate . . . a man no one can encompass without him being thrust forward amongst the ranks of geniuses.

To ᶜAlī ibn Abī Ṭālib I dedicate this Study of mine, which was written answering the inner urges and seeking a way to his blessings. There is something (in what I have written) which heals my soul of some of its burning thirst.

Personal Thoughts

Is it correct, my lord, that instead of making frequent visits to you, men disagreed about you?

Some of them have lost you and have not found you.

Some of them have lost you and then have found you.

Some of them have found you and then have lost you.

It is indeed incredible!

Fourteen centuries, with their hours, days and years have dissolved like the grain of salt dissolves in the palm of the ocean. Yet not a letter of your great name has dissolved. So how is it possible for these people to lose you and not find you, or to find you and then to lose you? O what an irony of fate! How do you consider the terms in which, even the people who have found you, portray you?

The words which have come from your lips have constantly refused for fourteen centuries to be limited to time or place because they carry from you the light of true values of thought and the struggles for the reality of life. They cannot be confined to any one framework.

Words, which come from your lips, refuse to settle in any one domain. How, then did you feel when they limited you within a committee which deprived you of leadership and the pledge of allegiance which would link you with the Caliphate? How were they able to cram you between a beginning and an end? So your swaddling clothes were the shirt of ᶜUthmān and your shroud came to you at the hand of ᶜAbd al Raḥmān b. ᶜUthmān. b. Muljam.

How did they find such a standard measurement with which they could begin to divert attention away from you and according to which they could begin to measure you. You were of medium height, not tall nor short, broad shouldered, tending toward solidness but not fat. Your eyes were black, your neck like a silver ewer. You had two sinewed arms, not only for the sword but also for rooting out bolted iron doors.

How then could they embroil you in problems and incidents which became your scene of conflict like the wrestling ring becomes the scene of conflict for two wrestlers?

Thus they begin at the Battle of the Camel "ᶜAskar", with the disabling of an army and the killing of Ṭalḥa and al-Zubayr and they end at Ṣiffīn when the drama changes to comedy which ends in tragedy. Thus have borders been framed around you and your existence been surrounded by a wall. You, indeed, are handsome, not because of the blackness of your eyes but because of the fire in your perception, not because of the brightness of your face but because of the purity in your heart, not because of the slenderness of your body but because of the greatness of your character.

You, indeed, are the hero! Sword and shield become solid in your hands, not because of the sinews of your arms or the broadness of your shoulders but because of a superabundance which favours your heart and your tongue and then abounds in your two paths of behaviour and eloquence.

You indeed are the one who set the first path. You wove a shirt for the world but it was not woven on the loom on which the shirt of ᶜUthmān was woven. You fashioned a sword for religion but it was not fashioned from the metal of the sword of ᶜAbd al-Raḥmān b. Muljam, the lover of Quṭām.

You indeed are the one who initiated the public treasury for Islam and then sighed with its burden. You look down on the world beyond its boundaries and beyond its range. You carry in your hand the pages of the Message. You show them to men but not in the way in which they were shown at Ṣiffīn . . . You are a light whose flame burns beyond the hump of the Camel and the flowing of the Euphrates, so that it crosses from Mecca to Medina. Not only does it cross to the deserts of Northern Arabia and the deserts of the Empty Quarter but it goes beyond that to the sun where it first appears and where it finally descends at its setting.

If those who have lost you, and even those who have found you, if they had realised that you are the towering figure, even though short in stature... if they had realised that your face was the colour of sun, even though made from clay, they would not have tried to describe you in mundane terms and they would not be able to realise, up to this very day, that they could thus lose you.

An Introduction to ᶜAlī b. Abī Ṭālib

I wanted to preface my introduction to ᶜAlī b. Abī Ṭālib with those personal thoughts. I feel that entering in his presence is no less sacred than approaching the prayer niche in a mosque. I am aware of the difficulty involved in every attempt to make the written word capable of portraying such a noble face because, while it is easy to portray something in its outward forms, it is difficult to get beyond the outward appearance to the true nature.

The reality of ᶜAlī b. Abī Ṭālib lies in his true nature rather than in his outward appearance. The difficulty which words have to portray him is no less than their inability to get to describe his true nature.

He did not come to this world like ordinary people, in their multitudes, come to it. For people come to this world to fulfil the ordinary goals of life and travel from it according to destiny and vanish after their allotted span amid waves of forgetfulness.

As for him, he came to this world as if he was bringing it. When it came to him, he remained as if he had overcome it.

If the written word was only satisfied to portray him in terms of the period between cradle and grave, it would be just a tool which deals with the outward appearances of things apart from their inner reality.

The difference between outward appearance and inner reality is vast. The ʿAlī, who was born in Mecca, lived six decades and died in Kūfa, is not the ʿAlī whose swaddling clothes were the Arabian Peninsula and who has continued to live for fourteen centuries without knowing the touch of the shroud. The ʿAlī who was content to live his daily life in old rags is not the ʿAlī who was not content with the leftovers of life.

Whenever the written word is content to portray him in this outward form, ʿAlī b. Abī Ṭālib appears drier than a sand dune scorched by the midday sun. Mecca is the place of his birth and Holy Najaf is the resting-place of his body. And he who was always dressed in old clothes. Yet amid the sand dunes scorched by the midday sun is an oasis which thirsty souls long for . . . between Mecca and Najaf there are oases which give shelter to generations of men . . . amid the wrappings of old clothes is a cloak which can only be worn in Heaven.

Even though ʿAlī's travels were limited for a short time between Baṣra and Kūfa or between Mecca and Medina, that never prevented him from being also that great runner whose footsteps went further than the halting places for caravans.

However much writers may describe him with pens which exaggerate or by which prejudices are made manifest, his heroism, although being more outstanding in their writing than the heroism of legendary characters, remains far weaker than its reality. For, it is of the kind which the words of writers are unable to describe because writing which deals with outward appearances without penetrating to their inner reality, remains writing which longs for true meaning like a person at the mouth of the well longs for its inner stores of water.

So every statement about ʿAlī b. Abī Ṭālib which confines him to place or time, will remain only an account which has some value as a report and it will exist as limited words which do not penetrate into the inner meanings.

How many are the pens which have dealt with him in this kind of weak reporting! They confined him within words. They have only been able to write about him in the context of Mecca and Medina, as if his vast range could not go beyond the area in which were Badr, Uḥud, Khaybar and Ṣiffīn . . . as if his strength could only be considered as being of the kind which the genie of the lamp can perform.

Such narrators become lost when they mix up strength with heroism and substitute one for the other in their description.

The reality is that his heroism was of a unique kind. It could not only root out the gate of the fortress of Khaybar but also the fortresses of ignorance in their entirety when their dark nights emaciate the minds of man.

All this I can summarise by saying that it is nonsense for us to connect the genius of a man like ᶜAlī b. Abī Ṭālib with the intricate mesh of events which miserable circumstance scattered around him as the winds scatter the clouds in the sky.

He did not will the events which passed over him but at the same time they did not change, in any way, the essence of that metal in which his outstanding personality was enclosed, just as the clouds themselves which cover the sky cannot, in any circumstance, put out the light of the sun.

Thus, these events are merely accidents. However intense they may be, however much the prejudiced intensify them, yet the essence of ᶜAlī b. Abī Ṭālib will remain beyond them just as the sun remains beyond the clouds.

Therefore, I will endeavour as much as possible to escape from all writing which deals with the dry account of events insofar as inner meanings cannot be explained by comments and footnotes.

I will never enter the sacred niche of this noble master except with a reverend bow, the silence of meditation and the respectful attention of one who seeks guidance.

I will contrive to make my account of him in a form of songs of praise as far as my pen is able to do so; for songs of praise are breezes whose words are only sweet when they mention saints.

I ask pardon from ᶜAlī b. Abī Ṭālib if I do not do well, for he is the best of those who excel and the most generous of those who grant pardon.

I

BASIC OUTLINES

The Historical Situation

It is necessary, when the discussion is about a pivotal figure like Imam ʿAlī, to give an historical sketch about the land in which he was born, the environment in which he lived, the climate of the life which influenced his existence and the aims and the ideals which he lived and fought for.

All of that is intrinsically linked with life of every individual. The fact that ʿAlī b. Abī Ṭālib was a native of the Arabian Peninsula fourteen hundred years ago, necessitates a brief account of the land to which ʿAlī belonged.

The Arabian Peninsula

The Arabian Peninsula is vast desert area which stretches between the Syrian desert in the North and the Indian Ocean in the South and between the Arabian Gulf in the East and the Red Sea in the West. Deserts cover most of the area like the Nufūd desert, the Empty Quarter, the desert of Herāt. These stretch all along it from North to South.

The area along the western coast consists of the Ḥijāz in the North and Yemen in the South. The Ḥijāz constantly used to suffer from scarcity of provisions because of the little rain which fell on it. Among the cities of Ḥijāz were Mecca and Yathrib (later known as Medina). Near the latter was the Mountain of Uḥud and the Jewish settlement of Khaybar where there was a famous fortress.

The products of the Ḥijaz consisted of cattle which lived on pastures which were more like sand dunes or beaches than fertile plains. There were also dates and some small plantations. Trading in spices took place which brought the area in closer contact with the neighbouring countries in the North and the East.

Its inhabitants were mainly nomadic. It has long been considered that from the dawn of history they were a source of the human emigration which flowed into the surrounding area in the North and the North-West. From them came, consecutively, the different civilisations of Babylon, Phoenicia and the Hebrews.

Life for its inhabitants was primitive in accord with its meagre economy, insofar as such a primitive life was reflected in the style of living and all their intellectual activities. [This reflection may be inspired by the idea which maintains that the economic situation is the basis for intellectual life and the basis of every higher development. In the book there are several occasions when data is given which in one way or another is in agreement with this idea. We, when we believe in the connection between the economic situation and the other aspects of intellectual and social life, do not accept that idea. Nor do we consider the economic situation as the principal means of definition for every society and the basis for every intellectual and social structure. This is so because of the evidence that the cultural and intellectual revolution may begin with a people who are backward economically and make out of them pioneering leaders for peoples who are economically richer and more powerful as the history of Islam proves. (*Note inserted by the Committee*)]

In this area no change appears, during the passing of time, in the way of life. Nor is there any development in the intellectual style except in relation to the contacts available to them through those emigrations which they had undertaken where those had been possible. From these they began to acquire all of what they came upon and what they could establish.

Such a nomadic life, such a weak economy, such exposure to burning sun in this vast area could not provide the conditions of life which develop among richer, more populous societies. They lived as separate tribes, raiding one another in order to provide what they needed to sustain life. This act was known as "al-Ghazwa" in the time known as "al-Jāhiliyyah" i.e. the time of ignorance.

Out of this sprung a scattered dislocated society, to which there was no loyalty such as is understood by more deep-rooted societies. This phenomenon always appears in societies with a weak economy.

Their tribes which gave unity to their numerous units were the outstanding phenomenon of their social lives. The loyalty demanded by the tribes alone linked them to these tribes so that out of that sprung a continuous dedication to rivalry and conflict which, in successive generations, reduced the value of the great society in the land which is still referred to as the Arabian Peninsula.

Alongside that, there existed a sharp intelligence. Yet it was superficial in so far as it lacked the abilities which would enable reason to understand what would train it and make it a real force. Paradoxically, a society emerged which was weak in intellectual aptitudes and rich in individualistic tendencies.

The tribal divisions of Qaḥṭān of the South and ᶜAdnān of the North remained the great genealogical basis which gave protection to the tribal tendencies of the tribal groupings of Kahlān, Ḥimyar, Rabīᶜa and Muḍar which were branches of the two great divisions. It also gave protection to similar tendencies of the great tribes which sprung from these groupings such as Ṭayy, Hamdān, Madhḥij and Qudāᶜa, or Asad, Wā'il, Bakr, Taghlib and the other branches of the genealogical tree which is usually referred to as Rabīᶜa, Muḍar and Yemen.

Their religious practices were confined to the worship of gods like Manāt, al-ᶜUzzā, al-Lāt and Hubal . . . idols which had been gathered in Mecca behind the veils of the Kaᶜba. They were not inclined to invest them with much importance because of their intellectual inability to grasp philosophy which does not find a fertile ground in economically backward countries.

However, the circumstances which prevailed in the Arabian Peninsula, did not prevent it from having some towns in which some commercial activities flourished insofar as their economies and characters were more advanced than the rest of the areas of the land.

Among the towns which had this important commercial aspect was Mecca, the cradle of the Apostle of God and the cradle of ᶜAlī b. Abī Ṭālib.

The Birth of the Prophet

The birth of Muḥammad was a beginning and an end, the beginning of a new era, the end of an old era.

The fact was that it had been ordained that the Arabian Peninsula, which had been long absent from the field in which the existence of man as man had been established, was to receive in this field the wonderful birth of a great man. This man would lay down, in the field of thought, a programme which would compensate for the long stagnation in which that peninsula had been submerged in darkness for generations.

Out of the self-same land, the great Apostle brought his great Message to be, even beyond the Arabian Peninsula, a religion and a constitution, which would link it to the ideals of thinking man, which would create for it a civilisation comparable with the civilisation around it to the East and to the West . . . and which would then raise its society from nomadic tribal decadence to the level of sophisticated unity insofar as it was to be established on the basis of a productive and well-developed economy.

Under the care of the noble Prophet, ʿAlī b. Abī Ṭālib thrived. No sooner had he opened his eyes to the Message which was thrust before him than the hungry lad had greedily swallowed it up, equally understanding all its ideas and aims both short-term and long-term. He became part of it and it became part of him, as he was of what it was linked to. He considered it the substance of redemption for a people whom it would free from their miserable economy, whom it came upon in the abyss of primitive, out-dated traditions and whom it would separate from the deprivations of negative reasoning and values.

There can be no doubt that coincidences are many . . . for it happened that the son of Abū Ṭālib lived at a time which was the most dazzlingly auspicious which the atmosphere of the Arabian Peninsula had ever come upon.

The Prophet, that winged intellect, brought up a second man, who was ʿAlī b. Abī Ṭālib, another pivotal centre for the human intellect. For the Arabian Peninsula, this was good fortune with multiplied results because the two men lived at one time. The second only came to complement the first. The second was the halo of the first and the first was the structure of the second.

In reality, it cannot be denied that ʿAlī b. Abī Ṭālib, that shining created intellect, through constantly being associated with his cousin, the Apostle, was his first helper and his most excellent advisor in all his affairs concerned with protecting the new Message and preparing for the means of its success. At the same time, the valiant struggler, that intrepid hero, acted in defence of it; it was defence by a believer who was firmly-rooted in knowledge of its correctness and the truth of acting on its behalf.

At first that was on behalf of the Arabian Peninsula . . . then it was on behalf of the Message itself, insofar as it would become – without doubt – the Message of the Arabian Peninsula for man wherever man could be found.

He was not one to proclaim the truth of what he was saying without being the first in whom the value of what he was saying was reflected.

The values of every word of the Message, which ʿAlī b. Abī Ṭālib proclaimed, after having shared in carrying it out, in producing it and in protecting it, he used to hear in such a way that those values were truly reflected in him, were closely connected to him in all his words and actions and all plans, both immediate and distant. He began to deliver it as a constant pattern for his own life so that through it he should be a living example for others.

In order to make ready a perfect society, he relied on the human personality being attached to virtues as a firm basis to which was guaranteed a sound intellect to understand, a sound programme to follow and a sound acknowledgement to declare.

The building of the personality of man through reason, ideals and personal qualities was the most outstanding undertaking of ᶜAlī b. Abī Ṭālib in the development of the Arabian Peninsula.

He began with himself. There is the value of the great. When I say "he began", I do not mean "he tried". Indeed the first rules which he embraced were basic to him. But now I have diverted to his intellect before putting them in a general perspective.

The Arabian Peninsula, which suffered from a surfeit in the vastness of its barren lands, used to suffer from a dearth of a human personality which could control these areas. It used to suffer from a dearth of human societies which such understanding personalities could have strengthened.

To this needed personality the Message brought all the required garments of knowledge. ᶜAlī b. Abī Ṭālib took all his own clothes from them. He brought them forward as apparel and attire so that he could offer them to his own people. Before them he appeared in the guise of one who offers. He wore these garments of knowledge through his understanding of the world and his understanding of the Hereafter. His abstinence from the former was a path to the latter.

He wore these garments of knowledge by virtue of his brilliant created intellect. He was power, will, courage, heroism and an ideal to be copied.

He offered these garments and was aware of the importance of offering them, but not heedless of all the obstacles which the ancient mental attitude of the Arabian Peninsula would bring against him, of all the prejudices of Qaḥṭān and ᶜAdnān which went back to their very origins.

He never felt that despair should be his lot because he saw things in a much larger perspective. What he was offering them would go beyond the temporal limits of his life. For this reason, he offered it without any attempt at cajoling.

In order to build this personality, ʿAlī b. Abī Ṭālib dedicated his life, firm in the belief that reason is everything in the existence of man.

ʿAlī b. Abī Ṭālib from an Historical Viewpoint

ʿAlī b. Abī Ṭālib b. ʿAbd al-Muṭṭalib is the cousin of the Apostle, Muḥammad b. ʿAbd Allāh b. ʿAbd al-Muṭṭalib al-Hāshimī.

The Arabian Peninsula was struck by a drought which ruined the great family. Muḥammad set about relieving the burden of his elderly uncle. So he took ʿAlī into his own family.

Ali grew up and thrived under the protection of his cousin, Muḥammad.

At this time Muḥammad was receiving revelation from the mouth of Gabriel in the cave of Ḥira. ʿAlī was the first to witness the birth of the new Message. At an early age, between nine and ten, he became convinced of the truth of the new religion.

He was early to mature, strong in build, sharp in intelligence, penetrating in discernment, brave and conversant with knowledge to high degree. He has left a great reminder of this in the book *Nahj al-Balāgha.* The Message put forward to public opinion the good news of the unity of God.

The leaders of Quraysh opposed it and considered it a repudiation of their own gods and a threat to the mandate of their leadership. From this came the beginning of the struggle which was gradually to increase from violence to greater violence and then to war and slaughter.

In all these stages ʿAlī was at the right hand of his cousin and his bravest and most useful supporter.

The emigration or *hijra* from Mecca to Medina was the first opportunity for the Message to escape from oppression. It gave Muḥammad a means of escape from the clutches of the leaders of Quraysh who were determined to kill him on one of the coming nights.

Therefore, ʿAlī b. Abī Ṭālib, in order to provide cover for the withdrawal of his cousin, slept in his bed so that the men stationed to kill the Prophet would think that the Prophet was still within their grasp. Thus he provided sufficient time for him to escape and get away under the cover of darkness, so that ʿAlī has been regarded as one of the first examples of self-sacrifice.

After the return of the emigrants from Abyssinia where they had been taken care of, the struggle began to take its violent form. The Battle of Badr was a first realisation of this and the Battle of Uḥud followed it. In the latter, victory was almost turned into defeat and the Prophet was wounded in it so that it was thought that he had been killed. The believers broke up. However, ʿAlī, by his heroism, achieved the final victory and with it the famous call of Gabriel was heard: "There is no sword except Dhū al-Fiqār. There is no young man except ʿAlī."

Other battles followed these two battles, the most famous of them is the Battle of the Trench, which is also called the Battle of the Allies because in it all the groups and parties with their different tendencies and tribes united to attack the Message which was advancing among the people. It resulted in violent force and a great victory for Islam.

The Battle of Khaybar took place at Khaybar, a Jewish fortress town famous for its solid gate, which Ali pulled down with the strength of his arm. The conquest of this town was the beginning of the conquest of the important towns in Arabia which started now to fall, one after the other, before the advancing might . . . until the conquest of Islam, in the name of the Message, prevailed in all the quarters of the Arabian Peninsula.

In all these battles, merit went first to the Emigrants because they were the first to answer the call of the Prophet in his emigration. Then it went to the Anṣār who received a return for their support.

The most famous of the first Emigrants is ʿAlī b. Abī Ṭālib. Many of them made a great contribution to facilitating the conquest and bringing about victory. However, ʿAlī b. Abī Ṭālib was absolutely the one who was most loved in the heart of the Prophet. He was his adopted son, his companion, his advisor, his constant lieutenant, his brother . . . the husband of his daughter, the dearest of people to him, Fāṭima the fair. Through Fāṭima he was the father of al-Ḥasan and al-Ḥusayn and the descendants of the Prophet were to be limited to her progeny.

ʿAli is the first of the believers, the strongest defender, the bravest warrior, the most resolute attacker and the most penetrating investigator of the truth.

The Prophet has referred to that with such statements as:

"O God, be a friend to whoever befriends ʿAlī and an enemy to whoever is his enemy."'

"ʿAlī is from me and I am from ʿAlī."

"Whoever has loved ʿAlī has loved me. Whoever has loved me has loved God."

"ʿAlī is with the Qur'ān and the Qur'ān is with ʿAlī."

"The rights due to ʿAlī from the Muslims are the rights due to a father from his sons."

"You are my brother in this world and the next."

"These two grandsons of mine (al-Ḥasan and al-Ḥusayn) are Imams, in times of ease and distress."

"Every son of a father traces their paternal relations through their father, except the two sons of Fāṭima. It is I who am their paternal grandfather."

The Prophet died and those who gathered in the hall of the Banū Sā'ida differed about whether the Caliph should be from the Emigrants or the Anṣār. The balance weighed in favour of the Emigrants and they recognised the right of the eldest. So Abū Bakr al-Ṣiddīq was appointed.

ʿAlī was absent from this meeting which was called the meeting of the hall of Banū Sā'ida. His absence was due to his preoccupation with burying the Prophet. He considered his rights to have been encroached upon because, according to the declarations of the Apostle, he had the most right to the caliphate.

Then after Abū Bakr, the caliphate was transferred over his head to ʿUmar b. al-Khaṭṭāb by the same argument.

When ʿUmar b. al-Khaṭṭāb died, eyes were turned to a consultative committee of six: ʿAlī b. Abī Ṭālib, ʿUthmān b. ʿAffān, Saʿd b. Abī Waqqāṣ, Ṭalḥa b. ʿAbd Allāh, al-Zubayr b. al-ʿAwwām and ʿAbd al-Raḥmān b. ʿAwf.

The final decision of appointing a Caliph was given to that last man. His choice was fixed between whichever of two men would accept the condition which he imposed, namely that whichever of them would agree not to appoint any of his supporters or members of his family to help in government would be the one who would be given control of the government.

By the virtue of the fact that ʿAlī would not accept the condition, the caliphate naturally went to ʿUthmān b. ʿAffān.

[ʿAbd al-Raḥmān b. ʿAwf had first said to ʿAlī: "I will pledge allegiance to you as Caliph on the condition of you accepting the Book of God, the *sunna* of the Apostle of God and the practice of the two Shaykhs (Abū Bakr and ʿUmar).

"Rather," replied ʿAlī, peace be on him, "I will accept the condition of the Book of God, the *sunna* of the Apostle of God and the use of reason."

ʿAbd al-Raḥmān b. ʿAwf went from him to ʿUthmān and offered him it on the same contions. He replied: "Yes." So ʿAbd al-Raḥmān returned to ʿAlī and repeated his words – he did that three times. However, when he saw that ʿAlī would not withdraw from what he had said and that ʿUthmān had given him a favourable reply, he took the hand of ʿUthmān and said: "Peace be on you, Commander of the faithful." (*Note inserted by the Committee*)]

The reign of ʿUthmān was a period of struggle between the Umayyad relatives of ʿUthmān and the family of Hāshim. Because of that the new Caliph could not find any way before him except to break the condition laid down by ʿAbd al-Raḥmān b. ʿAwf and to choose all his supporters from his Umayyad relatives.

[In fact history does not regard this as a struggle on the part of the family of Hāshim after the pledge of allegiance to ʿUthmān. Rather it sees it as a struggle between the Umayyads and the general masses of the Muslims, because ʿUthmān put the finances of the Muslims in the hands of Marwān b. al-Ḥakam and he showed preference to the Umayyads. These were among the things which led to the revolution of the Muslims and finished up with the death of the Caliph. (*Note inserted by the Committee*)].

At this time, Muʿāwiya b. Abī Sufyān was the governor of Syria. The conquest had brought about the expansion of the land of Islam and alluring economic prosperity to the Arabs. The fact that they were carried away by it was one of the causes for the dedication to division which had developed. The government of ʿUthmān b. ʿAffān had gone outside the texts of the Message and turned into an aristocracy which had created a new class. The fire of envy became enflamed among the tribes who had, before, been united in support of Islam. A revolution was born which led to the death of the Caliph.

Muʿāwiya, the governor of Syria, who had aspirations to achieve the caliphate for himself, opposed the new pledge of allegiance to ʿAlī as Caliph. This had been given to ʿAlī by the men of the Arabian Peninsula, who had rebelled against ʿUthmān, together with all the towns in the conquered territories, with the exception of Syria.

Bashīr b. al-Nuʿmān wrapped up the shirt of ʿUthmān and fled with it to Syria. Muʿāwiya kept the shirt and began to brandish it as a pretext for seeking vengeance.

Thus began the struggle on two fronts. ʿAlī was on the one side and with him the family of Hāshim and the Anṣār. Muʿāwiya was on the other side and with him those who were ambitious for the caliphate . . .

Out of this arose the affair of Ṭalḥa and al-Zubayr.

ʿĀ'isha, the mother of the faithful, was a firm supporter of her brother-in-law gaining power, out of love for him and hatred of ʿAlī because there was a long-standing antipathy between them. Muʿāwiya was favourably disposed to such an attempt. The Battle of the Camel took place under the leadership of ʿĀ'isha. However, the battle ended in defeat. In it Ṭalḥa and al-Zubayr were killed and ʿĀ'isha was taken prisoner but she was treated with tenderness and respect.

The struggle was left to intensify between the two main proponents (ʿAlī and Muʿāwiya). The Battle of Ṣiffīn was almost the deciding factor in favour of ʿAlī, if it had not been for the deceit in raising copies of the Qur'ān and in the arbitration of ʿAmr b. al-ʿĀṣ and Abū Mūsā, which led to a decision to remove ʿAlī and not Muʿāwiya . . . contrary to their agreement to remove them both and return the matter to the decision of a committee.

The war continued after the outbreak of a new front, the Khārijites, who revolted against ʿAlī for agreeing to the arbitration. He destroyed them at the Battle of Nahrawān.

ʿAlī was unable to accomplish anything against Muʿāwiya. This finally led to the agreement for a temporary truce in which Syria was left detached and ʿAlī continued to deal with affairs of government in Kūfa.

The conquests had become moribund as a reaction to this violent struggle which ʿAlī b. Abī Ṭālib had not been able to bring to an end. Then, one day as the Caliph ʿAlī was going to the mosque at Kūfa, ʿAbd al-Raḥmān b. Muljam suddenly struck him a blow with a poisoned sword which destroyed his life.

The Personality of Man

When a personality is formed, it is up to reason to give the general conception of the kind of structure which arises. It is that by which the paving of the foundation is completed so that the building may stand on it . . . whether it is tall and strong, adorned with colour and beauty or whether it is humble, faded and shrunken and will not last in any circumstance. For reason, and nothing else, is the inner meaning of man. It is the essence without which it would be impossible for man to live on the surface of the earth. It is as if it is the final quintessence in the furthest one of the chains of purifications which stretch throughout the length of life. It is as if it is the value which begins in the bitterness of the dust and sand of matter in order to attain in the end the purity of the spirit. It is as if it is the fragrance which follows the chain from the dust of the soil to pass over the colours of flowers into the lightness of the mind.

This reason, distilled from the substance of the body as wine is distilled from the grape, as scent is distilled from bunches of aromatic plants, is that which leads to thought just as wine leads to intoxication, just as scent leads to fragrance.

Reason, then, is that craftsman which only exposes the area of its crafts within the areas of its skill and the glory of its creations are only effected when these come into contact with the fascination of its astonishing creation. As a result it is that source of reference which the personality of man will only find when it takes refuge in its shelter. Then reason will work to develop that personality with all the power it has been given to develop it. Thus when the personality emerges from reason, yet still with reason's grasp, it is as if the personality is a true expression of the power of the noble character of reason, i.e. it arises out of reason to the limits of the heights of consciousness and of the depths of purity.

That craftsman, which is reason, is similar in condition to the builder who is devoted to the building he is engaged in; for its sake he frequents the quarries which he knows; he has sculpture and the polished stone on it; he stores for it materials from wherever he can lay his hands on them and whatever engravings, ornaments and equipment which he thinks appropriate for it.

As soon as his work stands completed before his eyes, he sits in front of it pointing to it . . . Here is the labours of his own hands. As for the building, it is truly a reflection of those labours. In the eyes of a critic the reality may be a miserable hut which will shake with the first wind, or an ordinary house which is familiar to poverty, or an elegant palace adorned with colour and opulence, or a huge castle which mocks the roaring storms, or a dignified temple to which generations may submit themselves to pilgrimage over the course of time.

Perhaps the architecture of the building became muddled and parts of it would interfere with each other. Then its colours would clash and struggle with each other, or its forms would clash with each other and be incongruous, or its walls would become feeble and twisted, or its halls would become bent and contracted, or its verandahs would dwindle and decrease . . . All of that would take place where it had been pleasant and where it was preferred that it should be glittering and in harmony, or it should be in proper association and in accord, or it should be delicate and round, or it should be square and spacious, or it should be rectangular and commodious.

It may be that the whole of its architecture does not get muddled . . . but the confusion only affects some of its engravings and the muddle only affects some of its equipment . . . Then the distortion would still extend to it and take away some of its value and detract from its splendour.

Yet perhaps it may be that he persists in giving effect to its architecture in the best possible way with that rare symmetry in which buildings and concepts are married together. Then, indeed, it would be well-proportioned and integrated; its paving stones would be overhung by its verandahs; its steps would glisten with its splendours; its hall would incorporate all its halls; its balconies would radiate with glorious light; and its colours would arise out of its diversity.

That is the ideal building by a great architect whose insights pervade his designs and whose wishes are absorbed in his efforts.

According to this measurement, the personality of man is transferred into its proper sphere as a result of reason. As for the quarries which it frequents for material in the course of its development, these are the merits and qualities which it gathers for itself handful by handful, sometimes parsimoniously, sometimes easily and sometimes abundantly.

Thus there is a gradual development from a poor personality with no existence outside the bodily substance, a doll which falls when it attempts to crawl, into a humble personality which humbly resorts to its temples with the trepidation of rabbits scurrying to their holes as they nibble the grass with their teeth; they hide from the day in the night and the light of their sun is put out with the opening of the buried graves. And so, into a haughty personality which borrows its colours from it and glories in its ancestry, imagining that it is easily distinguishable when in fact it is dissolving into its own shadows. And so, into the martial personality with polished qualities and well-proportioned exterior, which lives today for tomorrow and whose memory sprouts from its tomb. And so, into the personality with strong qualities, unblemished virtues and dignity which raises the earth to the clouds, which endows time with eternity, which adds beauty to the imagination, which covers tombs with eternity and which abnegates destruction through eternal existence so that it achieves the man through the man.

These are the stages of the personality of men. Among them is the paltry and insignificant man whom life only speaks of at its very edges. Among them is the poor miserable creature who is weighed down by the burden of his yoke and only welcomes his existence today out of fear of tomorrow. Among them is the rich deluded man who advances noisily to the shore expecting that the sea will surrender its secrets to him. Among them is the shining talented man who dallies with the sun even though it is behind the clouds. Among them is the chosen man, through whom qualities are revealed and in whom all true values are gathered together.

The Personality of ᶜAlī b. Abī Ṭālib

It was in that excellent metal that the personality of Imam ᶜAlī was clothed completing all the values of such a personality. It was a personality in which reason stood out as the absolute master. Indeed it was related to reason in the same way as rain is related to the clouds; it sought reason and reason poured down upon it in complete harmony with it. Thus the flag of reason was stretched above this personality and it made its leadership subject to reason. Each absorbed the other, force for force, colour for colour . . . until it was as if her strong structure was like the steel which only gathered all its elements together so that they should be a formidable base for a formidable leader.

Sword in hand and flashing in attack, he had two edges – an attacking edge which strikes against the shield and an edge which marked his ideas on paper – both of which were operating in one eternally pure way of giving help which had two principal aspects: towards struggle and towards guidance.

The dual nature of his acts of heroism was because the divine unity brought them together. Thus they coursed along in the field just like the currents course along the streams while still keeping to them. Yet it was streams of gifts which were clothed in virtues and qualities like the leaves of spring clothe the trees. These were closely interrelated in their harmony and mutual relationship like the beams of the sun, which is alone the source and like the furnace in which the minerals are melted.

Thus in this personality the sum of gifts, the sum of qualities and the sum of virtues have been fused, value with value, weight with weight, ability with ability. One is interwoven with another just like colours are interwoven on the canvas of an artist. These gifts are like a flood; they dart along as if in a race and they support one another like partners.

Integrity and truth are two gentle qualities which have great power with him through the support of his shield and his sword. Asceticism and generosity were two gentle qualities which he gave shelter to. Whenever they might become separate to any extent, they were reunited in him. Thus asceticism from the world was generosity to it and generosity attained its perfection through asceticism.

Piety and faith are two inner feelings and two pure springs which were zealously cultivated by him and which poured from his tongue. Indeed they were both for him a sword raised in defence of the Kaᶜba and in his piety there was a signpost to Islam.

Right and justice are two closely related qualities, two rare necklaces, two shining wings, which emanated from his conscience, which were adorned by his illustration of them and which were established by his spear. Indeed the inheritance of the values ranging between right and justice is to be found in his faith.

Love and sincerity were two firm bonds and two generous outflowings which were interlocked by his heart and tongue. Indeed through these collections of virtues the world gains warmth so that it can continue to seek its way.

Determination and resolution are two resultant outpourings from two mutual supporting qualities of steadfastness, strength and will. It is as if they are reflected from his eyes into his arms and burst forth in his policies. Indeed religion and the world, in his eyes, are two forms which seek the completion of the unity of existence from his two limits in every sphere.

Such are the gifts and the qualities which the personality of ᶜAlī b. Abī Ṭālib has drunk. Indeed in the existence of man they are a pillar to which the value of man adheres.

Lines to the Land of the Arabian Peninsula

O Arabian Peninsula,

Do you sleep in hunger and are you content with the poetry recited on your mountain passes which caravans cross laden with perfumes?

What do you care of deserts whose sands thirst for water, are ablaze with heat and are never quenched with water?

O desert of Nejd, O desert of the Empty Quarter, come close . . . Come close and gather yourself up. Only the gentle breezes will assuage the venom of the vicious heat. Only the oceans which lap your shores will bring coolness. Yet your shores are indeed places of abundance. O how often have your distant generations travelled to them!

Those were your recalcitrant urgings across the years to bewildering emigrations which did not move forward so long as you clung to your civilisation.

Come close and take something of what you have given, raid for raid, O wilderness.

Gather up the hems of your long night before the sleeve of this pure dawn.

Enjoy your fortune because on that day Mecca was your tender loins which witnessed a birth which your burnt deserts have never before witnessed.

Make your ablutions with myrrh and frankincense from among your perfumes and gather them as trails of your goodness. The time has come for you to burn them in your true atmosphere.

Give blessings to the multitudes through the pains of your labour because he who is born is the first born who will dismember you, yet will bind your earth to the sky above and will radiate light over your whole area.

Sweep the Kaᶜba clear of your idols. The magnificence of the belief in the One God has thrown the false gods of al-Lāt, al-ᶜUzza and Manāt into confusion.

You have brought about the union of the tribal divisions in your land of Qaḥṭān and ᶜAdnān. You are since the hour of his coming the central focus for millions. Towards you the eyes of countless visitors will be directed.

Yathrib, support of the Anṣār and wakeful guardian of the Emigrants, shine with the tribes of Aws and Khazraj. Clear the dust from your eyes. The dawn brings you good news of a light whose compass is such that your deserts will never be able to limit its horizons. It is a Message with the power of the flood. Its origin is without beginning and its extent is without end.

If you try . . . and what harm is there in trying? Defeat like the defeat of Uḥud will not affect its blazing radiance. It is a light which transcends the compass of limitation because its origin is more distant than place and more remote than time.

Seek guidance and the guidance pours out before you. Be a firm support, be a shrine. The support of the minaret will not harm you. Do not play with tourist attractions, for you will be using your talents indiscriminately. Then the threads of the mantle in which you are wrapped will become ragged and you will be disgraced. Preach unity and be one. The word has begun to fill the world as it resounds in your eyes: "God is the greatest," those words *Allahu akbar*. Look into the distance. A feeble eye will never lead your feet along the road which stretches in front of you because the forms of the letters will be too difficult for a creed which has escaped from its inner meanings and the clouds of imagination will never be able to grasp them.

Therefore, let them carry you to where you will find a man and provide for his growth. Be a vehicle for him, keep the road serviceable and appreciate the value of what you are carrying.

O land of the Arabian Peninsula, throughout history that will be the most magnificent of your caravans and the most fragrant of your perfumes.

The Birth of the Message

What is the concern of those who come in group after group? Do you think that the Word has captivated them? The Word was spoken only to be met with contempt and mockery as if it was idle talk. It was regarded worthy only of being rejected and suppressed as if it was blasphemy.

Black night was only a veil by which two scattered emigrations might be covered as if they were acts of theft which secretly skulked away.

To what are they coming while woe and exile are dragged equally across the speaker of the Word and the one who accepts it? What is the value of the Word by which a man may be taunted into isolation? When did Mount Ḥirā' become the Kaᶜba of the Arabs and of Mecca and Medina? How is such impudence possible from a cave? Who indeed are these men who are coming? When was it possible for the youth of the people to look down on the chiefs?

The well of Badr witnessed the first battle between ruler and ruled. In it the value of the Word was established between the ruler who began to be worried about his destiny and the ruled who began to display enthusiasm for his destiny, between a group who saw in the continuation of their state a perpetuity of their praise and a perpetuity of their well-being and a group who had come to feel a new firebrand which would remove temporary injustice and persistent humiliation from their backs.

The Battle of Uḥud did not end without the Word returning more strongly and more fiercely unyielding. Indeed it held fast to its meaning just as proof holds fast to logic. The weak cling on to a new hope just as a drowning man clings on to a rope of rescue. Indeed the Word was winged with goodness and truth; it radiated justice and beauty and it revealed visions adorned with ultimate reason and extended by imagination to destinations which captivate souls through the scope of their high ideals.

It is a Word which contains within its folds the palpatations of love just as its letters are moved by the dew of heavenly gardens.

Indeed the greatest God is the God of Moses, of Pharaoh, the God of Jesus and Muḥammad . . . a powerful God Whom existence clothes just as He clothes eternity and perpetuity. Destinies are merged in Him as horizons are merged in the air. Beginnings are unified in Him as are the lines of circles incorporated into each other. He is a compassionate God who takes into his lap the poor of the world . . . Muḥammad gathered these poor from the clutches of the lords of Quraysh just as before Jesus had gathered them from the tyranny of the Roman despots.

The Word tears open its horizons just as morning rips open the darkness of the night.

The cave was an opening out of which poured the blessings of light. The recesses of the Kaʿba were in despair at it. The jugular vein of Hubal was twisted by it and the visitors fell down confused and overcome. A feeling had drawn them before understanding had come to them. It was as if they were in bewilderment from it . . . feeling warmth as if it brought relief to one perplexed by his destiny.

A veil is removed . . . A curtain falls . . . The reality at the unveiling . . . A new Message . . . A new man. Those are the dregs of men, the poor of the world who grope for their faces after rubbing them in dust. Then suddenly they are faces raised anew before the sun. The value of man in his existence and his destiny has been reinvigorated in it.

Man searches for his path with his feet and he decides his destiny with his will . . . It is the freedom of a freed slave . . . No chains will oppress him and no slavery will humiliate him.

Just as the effects of victory at the well of Badr were of assistance to the effects of the defeat at the Battle of Uḥud in the same way the Battle of Uḥud sought protection from its effects from the victory at the Battle of the Trench. The enemy's cries for help at the Battle of the Trench to the fortresses of Khaybar were of no avail because the cave of Ḥirā' had become that distant echo.

It was time for the rulers of Mecca and the Kaʿba, full of idols, to be submerged beneath a reverberation which resounded through the air of the Arabian Peninsula only to go beyond it to East and West . . . to wherever men exist, to wherever place and time extend.

The Value of the Message

O Cave of Ḥirā' . . . Wouldn't you say that you were a store of flame? What precious voice has issued forth from you? It was not light like the air nor fragrant like the blossoms. The air which envelops the earth is – for all its lightness – heavier than it. It rests upon the air and circles in it. It is the scope of the existence of the blossoms with which the profusion of branches are weighed down since through it they are supported and because of it they live. Did the Word have this circulation from you?

It is no wonder . . . . Only man heard him who addressed man in the language of man. Caves only raise their voices with the word with which a cave may be addressed.

It was from here that the measure of the Message came. Indeed it was not mere words which are perfumed with rhymes. Rather it was a clear explanation from which existence could look down on eternity. It wanders in its halls within the imagination. Draughts of beauty are drunk in its vast fields. For thought it is its place of travel and its place of return. For the soul it is its desires and its full compass. During life with its hardships it is the cloak of consolation. For life behind the veil it is the stirring of hope in good reward at the place of return . . . Wishes for good sprinkle the path to it with scent and the most fragrant virtues perfume its essence. These are virtues which only hearts can encompass. These are hearts which only faith can hold. This is faith which only divine unity can make firm. This divine unity is such that only reason can embrace it. It is a reason which is only bestowed on man. Man is the circle of existence and existence is God in the beginning and in the end.

That is the Message.

It offers itself on its wide palm; light, faith, conviction, truth, love, brotherhood, loyalty, purity and consolation.

This is the call to be answered. The depths gather it just as a grain of sand gathers a drop of dew. Indeed it is reflected in souls and minds. At one time it softens its palm as if it were tenderness, then it tightens its bridle as if it were firmness, then it roots out evil as if it were a storm. All that it does with the palm of a hand which is generous and an arm which defends. Indeed the struggle is a struggle which propagates conviction and a struggle which defends without relaxation.

When acts of heroism begin, faith will guide it to a certain victory.

[We notice that there are many sentences in this section which are tinged with a mystical ambiguity similar to the Ṣūfī mystics. A similar mysticism is found in the next chapter in the section entitled "The Perfect Equipment". It is very probable that the writer was not so much aiming at giving a philosophical understanding of existence and the divine problem as providing a splendid picture from the literary angle. (*Note inserted by the Committee*)]

The Reality of Events

The arrow which glided from his bow no longer belongs to the quiver.

That was the concern of the Message. No sooner did it begin to circle in the minds of the people than they seized hold of it as one of their rights. For them it was appropriate for every circumstance. They grasped it to the extent of their need for it. Yesterday, they were in need of everything which would equally free their souls and their bodies from a slavery whose dominion had been long and whose darkness had been intense.

In the beginning it was a feeling which glided rapidly to the mind. Then it became a need towards which the mind was driven. While in its first period it used to seek shelters in refuges and hiding places, it evolved into a shelter in which those who sought help took refuge. In its first stage it went between Mecca and Medina and seemed to creep along. Then suddenly it raced along with no fortresses being able to stop it. It never paused at the borders of the Ḥijāz. The lines of the deserts never diverted it. It was not Iraq alone which was waiting. Nor was it only Syria which was beckoning. Egypt, at the gates of Africa, had begun to prepare the pillars of the minarets. Iran, with the keys to the East, had begun to facilitate the passage for its crossings. Withdrawal was transformed into an opening out and a driving forward. Defence was changed into propagation and an admonition and then to a concentrated attack. From this point, the need became a persistent urge to rational organisation which would continue to drive the wheel in its proper gears.

A great deal of preparation did not precede that because the success, which was ensured by speed, had not been anticipated to this degree. The greatest surprises are, in their turn, the most intense surprises.

The man who brought the Message was himself removed from the scene to offer to his Lord the balance of his account on earth, without that removal being preceded by a warning. In addition to that the Message was still only freshly in its covers. Men had not practised it sufficiently and it was still threatened by many apostasies like the withdrawal at Uḥud and then the return. It was still seeking help from the leaders of Quraysh, those men who had only sought to slip away from their thrones under challenge. There were still the false gods Manāt, al-ᶜUzzā and Hubal mumbling in the dust of their broken fragment under the veils of the Kaᶜba.

The Message itself had not yet been established in its polished form. There were still sayings of the Prophet scattered among the Companions, which had not been properly collected and arranged. In addition to all that, it was exposed to attempts to soften it under the numerous currents of reasoning and interpretation based on interests and whim.

At this very time, the young Message was groping for a path to resume its journey towards its distant goals.

[Where the writer says ". . . the man who brought the Message was removed from the scene . . . without that removal being preceded by a warning . . . ", the fact is that it was preceded by repeated warnings from the Prophet. There had been complete preparation and comprehensive planning to guarantee the integrity of the revolutionary experiments which Islam practised. The Prophet, may God bless him and his family and grant them peace, had announced several times in his last year that he was on the point of being summoned by God and answering Him. In his sermon at Ghadīr Khumm he defined the way forward for the experiment after him. On one side he linked it to the Qur'ān in its capacity as the highest theoretical reference for the Message. On another side, he linked it to the apostolic leaders who were at the level of taking on the huge responsibilities of leading the experiments infallibly, sincerely and with a proper awareness. Of those men, Imam ᶜAlī was the person who was equipped to do this through the stipulation of the Apostle to receive these responsibilities directly after the Prophet. The dissolution and random action which occurred after the death of the greatest pioneer, the Prophet, was not the result of lack of preparation and prior warning, but only the result of deviation. (*Note inserted by the Committee*)].

The Role of ᶜAlī b. Abī Ṭālib

Please forgive, ᶜAlī b. Abī Ṭālib, for you are with regard to the Message like the axle of a mill. The paths which you walked along in the company of the Apostle bear witness to the gravity of your step. For several years he walked along them alone with only you at his side also sharing in the unity of life, the unity of destiny, the unity of direction and the unity of thought.

What struggles of his soul did you not share in, O close companion of the path, the life and the struggle, with all the roughness in the path, with all the hardships in life and with all the burdens in the struggle?

O lover who descends on the heart of his loved one like fulfilment descends on the ardour of love . . . O half who shares with his other half in every task and misfortune . . .

When you slept in his bed, what difference was there between your garments and his cloak? Is there a unity of spirit closer than the urge to sacrifice oneself for another? No wonder, O loved one of the Apostle, that in his eyes you are like a streak of light which embraces two halves. He is one half of it and you are the other. In his view you are the gateway of knowledge while he is the city of knowledge. You are the husband of his daughter, his own flesh and blood, Fāṭima, mistress of the women of the world together with Mary, daughter of ᶜImrān. You belong to him like the heart belongs to the body and the pupil belongs to the eye.

What thought came to him without its drops falling on you? What resolution did he make without its burden coming into your arms? What sword did he draw without it being sharpened on your whetstone?

He only wanted to offer his noble soul into your hands while he was sending it into the lap of his Lord. Thus were you blessed with close companionship alongside munificence. Thus did you collide with discord at the pain of his departure.

So prepare yourself. The Message, which thrived in the shade of your heart and was served with the abundance of your discernment, will continue to link the belt of your sword with the vastness of the desert because you are the man capable of it when its vast spaces sink within it.

II

THE PREPARATION

The Influence of the Message

How were those embers which glowed from this narrow aperture and by which this silent mountain breathed, to subside?

Did they spring from little sparks produced by rubbing to leap into space like burning furnaces of fire?

That was the state of ʿAlī b. Abī Ṭālib when the inner flames were subsiding in his depths.

However, the Message, into which he poured himself and which poured over him, was the unique spark in inflaming his inner abilities just as it was the great electric charge which gave them power.

I use a single word when I say "Message" but it is a word much longer that the sum of its letters. It is the length of a bow, one of whose ends is planted in the earth while the other soars beyond the finite and the tangible. It is the bond which links this world with the Next and man with this day of his with man with his tomorrow.

What man does not have two days, a day of staying and a day of travelling? The first is the link to the second. Yet the link is weak and the future lives on in the immortality of existence.

Since the matter is like this, it is necessary to have some concern for the first day because it is the threshold to the second and because the load which is prepared for it is what it will take across to the other.

As for that second day, whatever its nature may be and however vague its description and definition may appear, there is no escape from the fact that it is coming. As for the equipment which is prepared for it, it must be prepared since then it will be available either to receive it or to be able to loose its wrapping.

Man, in his present day and in his coming day, is the first born son of life. Its inheritance is concentrated in him. He, alone, is the rising vigour which makes possible the realisation of development. He, alone, is the reasoning power which is capable of deriving benefit from the resources of existence. He, alone, is the discerning ability by which problems are solved and secrets revealed. Consequently, he is the kernel of society . . . Society for which he is its greatest framework and its impregnable shield and its finest realisation.

Since man is the first born son of existence, he revolves in the lap of this existence and does not foray into any other . . . the beginning of it and the end of it.

The method, alone, is hidden and it will only be attained by reason. In any case, the obscurity of the method does not prevent the attainment of what completes it. Despite all that, it may be attained by discernment and reflection.

Necessity is not something which "how" prevents, nor "why" changes, nor "when" delays, nor "whither" moves. Faith increases the beauty of compliance without doubt reducing its importance.

With this faith ʿAlī b. Abī Ṭālib prepared his baggage and the people's baggage for the crossing from one radiant day to a day of eternal radiance. With this great positive philosophy, he began to prepare the equipment to build an excellent society which would be made firm by man and in which man would be made firm by virtues.

The Visitation of Death: The Death of the Prophet

In what furnace would fuel be gathered for the cleansing of the soul? Is it in pain alone that such a cleansing takes place? What is the value of love? What influence does deprivation have on it?

There may be questions but the answer is like a process of fusion. For, the pain, which roasts the soul in the fire of its live coals, borrows its limbs from love and its elixir from bereavement. I use the word "limbs" so that I may give the words its property of beauty and I use the word "elixir" so that I may drink from the beauty of its sweetness.

Pain has a harshness and bitterness. Sometimes the soul may not find in anything else the quality in itself by which the two are transported into beauty and sweetness. Yet beauty may be melted and sweetness cooked. The soul presents them to the mind as a course by which some of its hunger will be covered.

This kind of pain came to ʿAlī b. Abī Ṭālib. That kind of beauty acquired possession of his soul and its sweetness was echoed on his tongue by that pleasantness of speech . . . Death alone is the watering place of eternal life. It brings bereavement to love.

In front of him, in his arms, beneath his eyes, the flame of life was extinguished from the heart of the Apostle. The brightness left his eyes. His arms let his hands slump down. His body was wrapped in the coldness of death.

How is a heart silent, in which the hearts of men have throbbed and to whose pulsation the ears of angels have listened? How does the light leave two eyes, from which the light itself has borrowed its splendour? How do two hands slump, on whose palms have been spread the burdens of the world and the joys of heaven? How does the cold of death cover a body which used to bring alleviation and peace to the world? Yet it is the reality . . .

ᶜAlī b. Abī Ṭālib came back from his bewilderment to believe it. It was there beneath his eyes in the coldness of death. He had been left by the man whom he most loved, the most intelligent, the most pious, the most exemplary. Right in front of him confident expectation and correct vision had gone into the slumber of eternity. The dear heart and the productive love had stopped in the awe of silence.

O Apostle of God, do you see whether it is the bitter end? Or is it the glorious beginning? And what of the Message . . . ? Do you see that it was withdrawn through your withdrawal to the cave of Hira? And what of the fields of strife? Where is Badr? Where is Uḥud? Where is Khaybar? Do you see that now they have been effaced from the land of the Arabian Peninsula? And what of the false gods Manāt, al-ᶜUzzā and Hubal? Do you see that they have murmured anew from their broken fragments to bring about now a retrogression into wicked joys.

Perhaps pain will not end as it cuts deeply into the soul of ᶜAlī b. Abī Ṭālib as he stands in front of the shrouded body in awesome silence.

Perhaps the intimate conversation of this great man to this the greatest slumberer in death will not end.

Yet he will seal his heart against this pain. He will seal it as a humble believer. He will cover these two eyes of his so that he may open those two other eyes whose lashes do not glisten with tears in front of death, which only see the present world for its harshness, which reflect that brief death is the escape of the prisoner and the shining goal.

The Visitation of Death: The Death of Fāṭima

However, the death of Fāṭima brought back to him the wound which he had sought to heal with steadfastness and faith so that it reopened it in love. The wound was ripped open so that blood flowed anew with another colouring. It is the colour of the earth with its flesh and its blood. The earth has a colour like the colour of bracelets and anklets, jewelry by which beauty is weighed down and by which coquettishness is increased.

The earth, even though its colour is the colour of chains, has imprisoned man so that he becomes familiar with it just as a wound would become familiar with its bandage. He becomes fond of it just like the cripple becomes fond of his crutch. He becomes entwined in it just like echoes are entwined with a phantom.

Fāṭima was warmth to the heart of ʿAlī and a bond to his world. Death did not separate her from him without him feeling profound emptiness and cold comfort. Behold he was face to face with the harsh reality of life – a wound and a bandage, lameness and a crutch, an echo and a phantom! Where is the watering place of heavenly comfort? His wound for the loss of Fāṭima was added to the wound for the loss of her father. He closed his eyes on the tears for them both and surrendering himself to true vision, he said: "You have hurried away and are close together."

The Field of Conflicts

Since pain has the same affect on spirits as the action of the whetstone on knives, so conflicts, in the same way, affect spirits like fuel under a cauldron.

The activity of arousal which conflicts have on spirits is not the same for all of them. The weak among them fall with frustration beneath their bullets. As for those who through them ascend the grades of maturity to the level of reason and true values, they are the ones who receive conflicts with defiance so that they provide them with the value of support.

The spirit of ʿAlī b. Abī Ṭālib was not merely of this kind. Rather it was the unique model which considered conflicts as spurs in the passage of life.

The conflicts which he faced during the course of his life, he did not meet with that jealous care which the people of the world show towards discomforts. That was indeed because he saw the world with a different vision from their vision. It was only a means for him while for the others it was end in itself. How great is the difference between the means and the end! The means is a tool whose value is necessarily small in relation to the value of what it leads to. The end is always more distant.

With this spiritual reality based on a creed with clear purposes, he dealt with the world, the whole world, with its conflicts and its tragedies. He derived benefit from them but it was a benefit from his own balance and texture. He made himself completely ready to meet the conflicts as a training by which he trained his soul. Even the death, whose bitter taste he experienced through the loss of the Apostle and then the loss of Fāṭima, enabled him speedily to endure its blows and transform them into their beautiful inner meaning. That meaning is what the Message announced in him insofar as he was clothed in it throughout his life and he reflected it clearly in all his words and deeds. Thus it was his asceticism, his piety, indeed it was the source of his defence of true values through that unique heroism.

The events which happened to him for quarter of a century after the Prophet's departure from the world were nothing but proofs of the firmness of his resolution in the face of such blows, without weakening his determination or reducing the steadfastness of his belief. Yet the events which preceded this period of time were no less influential on him, despite the fact that they were things which had passed while he was in his youth and had not yet accumulated, from the experience of time and the pressure of life, choice wisdom and high knowledge.

It is through delight of enumeration that the occurrences of these events will be looked at, namely those which fall within the orbit of conflict, so that the enumeration may give proof of the glory of the subject.

Islam: A New Religion

Essentially the most important of the conflicts which took place was not to the young man alone but to the Arabian Peninsula where it took place, or rather to the world, both East and West. It was a religion in which were gathered the true ideals of the unity of God in the light of reason which was capable of digesting the inspiration and stretched out a hand of need towards it.

It came to the Arabian Peninsula and it received it without attention. Why did the men of the Arabian Peninsula wander away from giving heed to their religion?

There is no surprise in that. There were a few carved stones in shapes which reason had not touched with its art nor the spirit with its translucence. They were not capable, in any circumstance, of loosening a morsel of humility and respect from those around them. That is not evidence that the desert did not want to have a religion. Rather, in another way, it is evidence that a reasoning religion had not worked beyond the reason of the desert. So there was the new religion. Suddenly reason awoke from its long sleep. The people embraced it after perplexity.

The conflict which weighed upon them was the kind of terror of one who wakes up to carelessness. He seeks to be ready through sleep and he is urged on through the lack of readiness.

At this time ʿAlī b. Abī Ṭālib was the first whose reason was capable of accepting the great call. He took hold of it with understanding and conviction. For him it did not constitute a conflict as it did for others. Indeed he took it from the reality of life as the equipment for life.

Therefore he defended it. For its sake, he slept in his cousin's bed on the first opportunity which he could take advantage of as testimony of his complete conviction in its truth. This opportunity which he took should be regarded on the level of self-sacrifice.

For its sake he travelled across the length of the deserts of the Arabian Peninsula so that pride may be achieved for the lines of the caravans of the Emigrants. To defend it, he launched himself into battle after battle with that rare courage which has put him in the ranks of the few heroes.

The Battle of Uḥud

The Battle of Uḥud brought a desire to suffocate the new child. The repudiation involved in it was distinguished by the head of a fox and the heart of a rabbit . . . it was twisted around itself as if it was a snake.

It was a conflict of reason with ignorance, a conflict of the heart with the weakness of faith, a conflict of consciousness with the limitations of vision. What determination can lose these valuable assets and still preserve for itself a glimpse of bravery or a modicum of will?

So it happened . . . The rumour of the death of the Prophet at Uḥud breathed its poison. Thus the bravery of the weak Companions was overturned into weakness and withdrawal where before the bravery of the believers had been multiplied and transformed into heroism.

That was the effect of these conflicts on those resolute spirits. As for ʿAlī b. Abī Ṭālib, he took advantage of that clash at the Battle of Uḥud so that he transformed it into the resounding cry:

> There is no sword except Dhū al-Fiqār;
> There is no young man except ʿAlī.

Indeed that repudiation, even though it carries its emaciation in its heart like the consumptive carries the germ of his disease, is at every moment oppressed by its defeats so that it plunges with them into battles with aspects of the act of heroism which it claims. Yet they always remain inverted acts of heroism which history curses and records in the chapter of destruction and ruin.

That kind of repudiation lived at Uḥud and lived in what came after Uḥud. How often did ᶜAlī b. Abī Ṭālib endure these clashes throughout the length of his struggles. He was always meeting them with the same origin and with the same level.

Battles followed Uḥud. Every battle intensified its greed for another in proportion to the strengthening of the Message at the hands of the Emigrants and the Anṣār.

In them the conflicts were transformed into a desire for booty because the concept of the Message had become clearer to those who defended and struggled.

The help which Anas b. al-Nadr offered was sufficient for Uḥud. If Muḥammad had been killed, the Lord of Muḥammad could not be killed.

Thus the struggle began to be transferred from its material form to its spiritual form: from a battle which craves for prisoners to a struggle which aspires to free prisoners; from a fight which brings heaven down to earth to a fight which raises earth to heaven; from a defence of Muḥammad without involving the Lord to a defence of Muḥammad who has the Lord of the heavens and the earth.

This spirituality brought about the heroism of Abū Dujāna al-Anṣārī. When the Apostle wanted to release him from his pledge of allegiance after the defeat of Uḥud, he wept in front of him and said: "No, by God, where should I go . . . ? To a wife who will die? Or to a son who will be lost? Or to a house which will be destroyed? Or to property which will come to nothing? Or to a fate which has come close?"

He remained and with ᶜAlī they were two wings in the battle until he was killed. Thus the ultimate victory was achieved for him.

The Battle of the Trench

The Battle of the Trench was nothing but one of those battles in which polytheism of every kind has banded itself together. Its allies were united in the diversity of their inclinations; they were united to confront the danger which had suddenly come upon them.

This danger was the kind of whirlwind which blows down dilapidated walls. However, the five years which had passed while the Message had been in Medina were only preparatory for the unbalanced number which gathered, for the disunited force which was mobilised. Indeed the power which appeared in the arms of ᶜAmr b.

ʿAbd Wadd did not have any of the measure of heroism which had come to the breast of ʿAlī b. Abī Ṭālib.

Thus victory in the Battle of the Trench was for the force which was strengthened by the clear truth and defeat was for the force inflated with atheistic unbelief.

This rule cannot be mistaken. He who defends truth and conviction is always in the ranks of the victorious. There is no difference, then, whether his victory be by a blow of the sword or by a verbal thrust from the tongue. Victory will always be there in the last battle.

With this strengthened force, the conquest of Mecca was brought about, then the tribe of Thaqīf, then the tribe of Hawāzin in a chain of battles. Later one group of them began to dwindle from another because after this period of time resistance had become for them a matter which was inverted from the affair which they had undertaken at the beginning. Even the repudiation of the Message had become cramped and its effect had become hidden in the depths of some of their souls instead of being clearly on their arms and bodies.

Essentially the repudiation was not the effect of the fight against faith because it was devoid of faith. If it acted, its action was only like striking in the dark without guidance because it was without objectives . . . yet even if it had had some objectives, they were mean and paltry, soon to evaporate through time.

This is a brief allusion to the most important events which occurred from the time the Message was put forward as a summons to public opinion among the people until the disappearance from the scene of the man who brought the Message. It is a period which was not long when it is measured by time but it was much more distant than the area into which it exploded. It had an effect like the effect of a spark in the heart of a volcano.

If we were to say that its effect was equal on all spirits, that would not be absolutely true . . .

Disparity was present even though similarity was close. Similarity alone unites the human race with everything in which their similarities are gathered. These are the shared uniting similarities like the eye or the hand. Every person has two eyes and two hands. Yet the eye in any man has distinctive characteristics from the eye of any other man, whose compilation and enumeration are not possible.

Are not souls appropriate for that and the views and inclinations which their world contain, which scatter them in many directions, such as things which limit them to the tangible and make them fly beyond that in a variety of directions, and according to the disparity of their powers, motives and supports, and whether reason controls them or they are lost from its restricting influences . . . to the furthest extent which is capable of making the removal of differences between man and man in the realm of the impossible.

However, that does not make impossible the existence of intellectual tendencies which alone will provide the crucible in which the views of men are fused so that their differences are brought close together, their ways are harmonised and their impulses are set aright along the path of unity of thought and power when that takes place in the best of human societies.

These intellectual tendencies acquire a miraculous nature to the extent of the values of the harmony with human need which they carry in their heart . . . To the extent of the validity of these values which they offer to man, to the extent of that, it is possible for them to accompany him in his life . . . whether from one day to another, or from one generation to another.

In this long interval man has been accompanied by the Message of Islam . . . He has been accompanied by it since that day. He will always be accompanied by it until the last Hour because it has enriched his needs earlier and it has enriched his needs later.

This concern to give the true value to the Message is something which was active in the whole being of ᶜAlī b. Abī Ṭālib. Indeed throughout the period which has been described he assumed the role of the leading proponent. The scene of action was never without him for a single day. Neither weariness nor exhaustion kept him back from appearing on it. Even inflammation was removed from his eyes in a miraculous way so that no inadequacy in undertaking any hardship could be reckoned against him.

All that may be summarised in the words: ᶜAlī b. Abī Ṭālib lived the Message from the moment he understood it. He met every challenge which arose in its path with the action of a resolute believer. Indeed at the last of these events, at the death of the Prophet, he was their very pivot towards which men's gaze was turned.

After the death of the Apostle . . . A trust is withdrawn and a trust is left as a pledge. The pledge is what was born yesterday and was expelled. Then it soon gathered itself from its expulsion and it became that unfolding of truth which was destined to be driven forward. The cost of it attaining this level was not little. War progressed along its path with the blood which was given to quench a violent thirst. Then, despite this diversion in its growth, it began to stretch its neck beyond the horizons of the Arabian Peninsula. Its situation was no longer the same as it had been yesterday. It shone forth from its noble balance heavier than all burdens, longer than life and further than place. Today it abandons the lap of the man who brought it to throw itself on the shoulders of those who grew in its lap. This is responsibility to its full extent and the extent is nothing but profound importance.

The case put forward has reached a level which deals with man in his life and his destiny; in his life as an individual and in his life as a society; in his destiny as a traveller from the transitory to the eternal. It then deals with life in all its philosophical aspects whether they be social or religious. It binds the former to the latter just as it binds the spirit to the body.

Who is the one who can sustain the responsibility, can fill the empty centre, can assume government and can take the helm in the ship which has spread its sails and began to move in the broad sea?

In this connection all the arguments, which arose at that time between the Emigrants and the Anṣār about who had the most right to the caliphate, were not put forward merely because of the importance of a position. That was the nature of its essential qualities and specific conditions in relation to society, the times and the Message dictated this nature.

What brought the confirmation of this right for the Emigrants in the first place was as a direct reward for what they had suffered and they were the first to suffer by supporting and defending the Message with their lives. Succession became the lot of Abū Bakr al-Ṣiddīq by the same argument which the Emigrants used against the Anṣār. Yet ᶜAlī b. Abī Ṭālib could have used it against his Companions, the Emigrants. He was the first of them to believe in the Message, the greatest of them in support of it, the closest of them in relationship to the man who brought it, and the most profound of them in understanding its content. Perhaps Abū ᶜUbayda b. Jarrāḥ was more anxious about ᶜAlī's future than ᶜAlī was for himself, when he answered ᶜAlī's objection with the words: "You are a young man. These others are mature men. Let them have it with their experience . . . If you live and time stretches ahead for you, then you will be both worthy of and entitled to this affair!".

ᶜAlī b. Abī Ṭālib faced this blow and withdrew before it like a noble man faced with wrongs. He did not stir up agitation as Saᶜd b. ᶜUbāda had done. Rather he began to collect together the parts of the Qur'ān and from it to sow on to his heart the stitches of its exposition. Then the death of Fāṭima, at this time, brought a second blow to him which brought forth in his soul great magnanimity.

In his speech known as *Shiqshiqiyya* he said: "So I endured while all the time there was a mote in my eye and an obstruction in my throat."

The same reason was used to transfer succession after the death of the first Caliph, by-passing him, to ᶜUmar b. al-Khaṭṭāb, another mature man from among the mature men of the Companions. ᶜAlī b. Abī Ṭālib submitted to a new situation and dealt with this new blow with the positiveness of a man of deep-rooted faith. He began to assist the new Caliph with all the solutions which were obscure to him. It was the assistance of man anxious for the future of a Message which was part of his heart just as it was part of his brain.

Ten years passed for ᶜUmar b. al-Khaṭṭāb. Their end came with a blow from the sword of Abū Lu'lu'a. Then came the turn of the third Caliph, ᶜUthmān b. ᶜAffān. In this the blow to ᶜAlī b. Abī Ṭālib was the worst and most violent so that it became later the most radiant in the crystal of his personality and the perfection of its maturity.

The Error of ᶜAbd al-Raḥmān b. Awf.

O sir, if you had known that the twentieth century still has the right to take account of a mistake which took place fourteen centuries ago, you would have been more careful in your choice of the man who was best to be given the reins of a government which dealt equally with the world and with heaven. That choice demanded much wakefulness from you and further consideration. Still, no member of the six-fold council which delegated you the task was less capable of bearing responsibilities towards the problems than you.

The task which was put before you did not concern you and the council any more than it concerned our own times.

The Message, itself, which had been the Prophet's presentation to his people, came out his most exalted compass and the compass of the Arabian Peninsula to become the property of mankind in all its different environments and the multiplicity of its generations.

Therefore, you had a duty to be heedful in the choice which you made so that the Message was not exposed in its cradle to errors which would reverse and obstruct its progress in its momentous advance.

When you linked destiny to an ephemeral question and an inconsequential answer, in what thing were you so deeply involved and from what were you trying to prevent evil consequences and the natural result of its destiny?

A responsibility had been thrust upon you, ᶜAbd al-Raḥmān b. ᶜAwf, to sound out views and to make the pledge of allegiance for the caliphate to the one most appropriate for it, if not to say the one most entitled to it and the one who was the most excellent.

You did not sound out the view of ᶜAlī b. Abī Ṭālib except about a condition which you imposed. You did not sound out the view of ᶜUthmān b. ᶜAffān except about a condition which you imposed.

The condition, in both cases, was a trivial condition which could not be an appropriate basis for the task for which it was put forward . . . Above all else, you knew both men very well. They had been your colleagues in a long struggle. The merit of the one and the lack of merit of the other did not escape you. You were not ignorant of the fact that, while the message united them both, the extent of their understanding of it distinguished them. You were not ignorant of the fact that, while heroism in battle linked them to it, one of them was far more outstanding than the other in his activity in that field. You were not ignorant of the fact that, while great enthusiasm possessed them both, one of them could be distinguished from the other by his creativity. Thus it was possible for you to see which of the two noble men could achieve more than the other in relation to his asceticism, his piety, his sincerity, his loyalty, his resolution, his boldness and his power and furthermore his ability to judge . . . or in relation to a tendency towards senility as a result of weakness of enthusiasm, or in relation to a tendency towards the totality of noble, chivalrous qualities as a result of strength of resolution.

All that should have been considered before you put your weak question: "I will pledge allegiance to you ᶜAlī on condition that you do not make any one of the family Hāshim master over the people."

"I will pledge allegiance to you ᶜUthmān on condition that you do not make anyone of the family of Umayya master over the people."

[In fact the condition that ᶜAbd al-Raḥmān b. Awf laid down was different. He demanded of Imam ᶜAlī and then ᶜUthmān, that each governed according to the practice of the two previous Caliphs, Abū Bakr and ᶜUmar. Imam ᶜAlī refused but ᶜUthmān accepted. See the Commentary on *Nahj al-Balāgha* by Ibn Abī al-Ḥadīd, commenting on the Speech *Shiqshiqiyya* (*Note inserted by the Committee*)].

It is clear that ᶜUthmān was removed from the claiphate because he consented to the condition. It is also clear that ᶜAlī b. Abī Ṭālib did not gain the caliphate because he refused the condition. The one who attained it accepted the bargain and the one who lost it refused the bargain. The scale weighs between acceptance and rejection.

You, sir! You laid down this condition of yours as an edict of conduct in the constitution of the state. However, ᶜUthmān b. ᶜAffān made light of your condition. He did not feel that he was committing an act of disbelief either to you or to his religion, because your condition was not religious in its requirements. Rather it seemed good to him to gather his chief lieutenants from all his relatives in family of Umayya. That would not have been able to harm him if they had not harmed him by deserting the truth path. Nor did they harm him alone but rather they harmed the Message which was still in its infancy.

As for him who was not willing to bargain, he was anxious for you to keep away from an unnecessary condition and for you to believe that he was the appropriate person to entrust affairs to. His concern was that they should be entrusted to a house which had already been implicity entrusted with an overflowing bowl of inspiration amid its furniture.

The condition was essentially trivial, ᶜAbd al-Raḥmān b. ᶜAwf . . . if there was no intention of conspiracy hiding behind it . . . The intention of conspiracy had the direst of consequences.

Between two Opposites: A Vacuum is filled

The period of twenty years which passed for ᶜAlī b. Abī Ṭālib, from the death of the Apostle to his finally assuming the caliphate, was not an easy period, neither by virtue of its length nor by virtue of the events which took place during it. Even though it could be considered a vacuum insofar as he did not carry any administrative responsibility, it was in effect a vacuum which was filled.

It should not be understood from the word "vacuum" that ᶜAlī b. Abī Ṭālib was absent from the scene during this long time. Indeed, on the contrary, he was in it in a way that filled it by ear and sight but he was only occupying the position of a watch-tower in it.

While ᶜUthmān's eyes were shut to true concern for the Message, Abū Bakr and ᶜUmar had made some attempt to understand it. At least in their time it had some measure of proper direction and implementation. Now it was administered by a state which laid its thorny path amid the old ignorant customs and practices of the past. Yet it began to encounter new growths which demanded much concern and caution. The powers of the state had become numerous after it had been slightly distracted in suppressing the movements of apostasy by which some of the tribes of Yemen, Yamāma and ᶜUmān had disturbed the peace. It had gone on to conquests in every direction.

From one side, Iraq was defeated and the city of al-Madā'in made known the treaures of its white palace. Saᶜd b. Abī Waqqāṣ sat in the courtyard of Choesroe. The land of Persia submitted to the Arabs, who began to knock on the doors of India.

From a second side, the gates of Syria were opened to ᶜAmr b. al-ᶜĀṣ, Khālid b. al-Walīd, Muᶜāwiya b. Abī Sufyān and Abū ᶜUbayda b. Jarrāḥ. Heraclius had been defeated and while departing had said his famous farewell: "Peace be on you, Syria! What a wonderful land. Now you belong to the enemy."

From a third side, the road to Egypt had been opened before the Conquerors under the leadership of ᶜAmr b. al-ᶜĀṣ and al-Zubayr b. al-ᶜAwwām. Al-Maqawqas had agreed to pay the poll-tax into the hands of the black man, ᶜUbāda b. al-Ṣāmit.

All these conquests had been achieved in the reigns of Abū Bakr and ᶜUmar b. al-Khaṭṭāb. Treasures and wealth poured into the state such as the history of the Arabian Peninsula had never seen before. A more intense and munificent raiding had never been known in the past than this raid of conquest, the length of whose fronts stretched equally from East and West and South. It was as if heaven opened up the streams of the rivers of Paradise and torrents poured down submerging the Arabian Peninsula in honey.

While Abū Bakr and ᶜUmar b. al-Khaṭṭāb were only nibbling at the world trying to avoid it and abandoning control of the conquests which swept through East and West on the slack-reined horses of defiance, Saᶜd b. Abī Waqqāṣ was sitting in the courtyard of Choesroe planning to build his own palace in Kūfa like it and collecting for himself all its treasures. The leaders were entertaining themselves with booty and prisoners. Al-Zubayr b. al-ᶜAwwām possessed a thousand male slaves and a thousand female slaves.

At this time of the expansion of the state, ᶜAlī b. Abī Ṭālib was stationed in his high tower beset by what he saw, taking about of it and asking himself: "Is it for the sake of all this that the Message was put forward?".

Did not God, the Exalted, say: *Piety is not turning your faces to the East and West. Rather piety is one who believes in God, the Last Day, the Book and the Prophets and who gives his money out of love of Him to those who have kinship, orphans, wayfarers, beggars and for freeing slaves . . . Those are the ones who are pious.* (II 177).

Was the expansion which took place and the state to which it was connected the realisation of the Message or was it still the vehicle of the period of ignorance? Wouldn't you say that the period of ignorance, whose outlines the Message had come to destroy, was dealing with the Message in such a way that it might return and pour into it? What influence did the Message have on the tribes of Ṭayy and Asad. What was wrong with Ṭulayḥa, the liar, whom the tribe of Ghaṭafān followed? What did Muslayma and Sajjāḥ have to do with prophethood, behind whom were drawn along the tribe of Ḥanifa in al-Yamāma and the tribe of Tamīm? What prophethood did al-Aswad al-ᶜAnsī claim to be answered by the tribes of Baḥrayn, Ḥaḍramawt, ᶜUmān and Yemen? If the swords of the Muslims had subdued these contradictory apostasies and the leaders had come within the fold, was that success in terms of saying that those tribes who had apostasised and then withdrawn from their apostasy had become convinced of the truth of the Message?

Was the conquest itself, which had poured over the boundaries of the Arabian Peninsula and then overflowed other boundaries, was it a really true conquest which the Message had in mind? As it says in the Qur'ān: *Do not enter houses other than your own until you become friendly and greet their families* (XXIV, 27).

Indeed God enjoins justice, doing good and giving to those who have kinship and He forbids adultery, wrongdoing and injustice. (XVI 90).

Accept repentance and enjoin the good and avoid those who are ignorant. (VII, 199).

Say, My Lord only forbids vile deeds, those seen and those within (VII, 33).

The noblest of you with God is the most pious. (XLIX, 13).

As the Apostle says: "One who calls for tribal loyalty or fights for tribal loyalty does not belong to us".

As He, the Exalted, says: *God buys from the believers their lives and their property by virtue of the fact that they will have heaven through fighting in the cause of God.* (IX, 111).

Those are verses which clearly explain the Message. None of them point to a right to acquire slaves in their thousands or to take up valuables in millions as a result of a profit-making war or a bloody battle. They do not permit the exploitation of people, the violation of their womenfolk and the enjoyment of prisoners. Rather they put forward the opposite of that . . . to save man from slavery, not to free him and enslave him in another way . . . to bring him back to the lap of his Lord as a free and dear person, not to make his bonds into chains for other men . . . to free him from the compounds of his weakness and from being dominated by the material.

Was this materialism a hunger which distracted his reason through his stomach or was it a satiety which made his reason be entertained by his stomach?

The awakening of reason to its full extent had been brought by the Message, not the awakening of the appetites to their full extent. It had come to wipe out tribal loyalties so that they may be united in one loyalty by which the Arabian Peninsula would be strengthened. It had come to build up the Arabian Peninsula, to make a sound man . . . then a sound society . . . then a sound release of true values.

Yet up to now the Arabian Peninsula had not been built up. In the view of ᶜAlī b. Abī Ṭālib, it was in need of the kind of building which would be concerned with its foundations . . . man first of all . . . and the ruler was the first man who had to be built.

You know that it is not appropriate for the ruler to be involved in lust and bloodshed, and to be mean with the laws and trust of the Muslims, for then his appetite will be for their property . . . Nor is it appropriate for him to be ignorant, for then he will lead them astray through his ignorance. Nor is it appropriate for him to be brutish, for he will cut them off through his brutishness. Nor is it appropriate for him to deal unjustly with states, for then he will show favour to one people apart from another. Nor is it appropriate for him to be corrupt in the law, for then he will take away their rights and stop them without conclusive evidence. Nor should he be inactive in operating the practice of the Apostle, for then he will destroy the community.

The task is not an easy one. The education of a people is nothing but a distant reflection which their rulers and leaders reflect through their ability and administration. The Arabian Peninsula was in need of such a broad schooling before its forces were called upon to undertake campaigns of conquest beyond its borders. Its borders were exposed to what they would have to fortify against later . . . The Message had come to fortify them. Here "fortify" is not meant in a military sense. Rather it means that they were not yet fortified with the fortification of mature reason and productive thought.

This is what was making the vacuum of its ignorance more extensive than the area of its land. Therefore, the conquests, which it undertook, constantly brought it military victory while no real spiritual victory was recorded for it except the Message which was capable of giving it precedence over the blade of its sword. Whenever that true structure was made possible in the Arabian Peninsula, then of its own accord it would abound in its environs with true conquests which brought about spiritual victory without any need of the sword but rather through the power of thought radiating with truth and justice. The sword could not achieve for the Message the kind of victory which reason, brought by the Message, could achieve for the Message.

All that ʿAlī b. Abī Ṭālib saw from his isolation. He saw the tribes of Ṭayy, Asad, Ghaṭafān and Tamīn acting in the former ignorant manner. He saw the path which the family of Hāshim and family of Umayya walked along as they tried to wrest it from each other in order to get to a throne under which were concealed the pride and accoutrement of leadership. He saw the conquests achieving different aims and bearing different fruits. He saw that the Arabian Peninsula, which was still slumbering in the night of its yesterday, had been woken up like a startled sleeper only to savour plunder and booty at the expense of the enlightened Message to such an extent that holy war had become a means to booty much more that a means of realising true goals.

All that he saw with the vision of an onlooker. He made ready protective equipment for it to take the instrument of administration when the reins of government eventually came to him. As for that equipment, it was adorned to the greatest extent with a resolute determination which could not accept any bargaining with truth. Thus was his affair restricted by the blindness of the advice which ʿAbd al-Raḥmān b. ʿAwf offered when the caliphate was handed to ʿUthmān b. ʿAffān.

Between two Opposites: The Filling is itself a Vacuum

Tribal bias brought this old man to the caliphate.

Slowdown, ʿAbd al-Raḥmān b. ʿAwf! You wanted it as a condition and it was like that! ʿUthmān b. Affān would only ever help to choose those men who had been well trained in the principles of the Message, whom the tread of events had blistered, whose minds and souls had become mature, who rejected the world as if it were meaner than a pip and who worked for the Next World as the blessed place of habitation and return for them!!

In fact, the man whom the Apostle banished because he used to write against him and because he doubted the truthfulness of his inspiration was the man whom ʿUthmān b. ʿAffān found most helpful to him in government. Therefore ʿAbd Allāh b. Abī Sarḥ became governor of Egypt.

Similarly al-Walīd b. ʿUqba, another man who merited the curse of the Prophet, was the man chosen for Kūfa to wait for him to fill the vacuum there and to organise its affairs and conditions.

Marwān b. al-Ḥakam was according to him the most well-groomed and able man who could be handed over the registers of state. The control of the registers of state had the greatest importance since they brought control over the direction of the state and its internal and external policies.

These were the officials whose duty was to supervise and oversee the centres of the state which had begun to spread from the borders of Armenia, Iran and Azerbaijan after passing through Iraq and the whole of the Arabian Peninsula to Cairo in Egypt and Dongela in Nubia even up to Tripoli and Carthage in the West, even as far as Cyprus and Syria and all the colonies of the Byzantine Empire along the shores of the Mediterranean. All these vast possessions could only be controlled by these men whom ʿUthmān could find from the family of Umayya.

This was your condition, ʿAbd al-Raḥmān b. ʿAwf, which ʿUthmān so cursorily discarded.

However, the importance of this matter was not only from that aspect. It went a great deal beyond that since the mere appointment of men from the family of Umayya to take over the administration of government was not something which would change the course of history. Indeed the men from the family of Umayya are like the rest of the leading personalities among the Arabs . . . Muʿāwiya b. Abī Sufyān was the great standard of family of Umayya and one of the leaders with such cunning and craftiness as is rarely seen in history.

It was not a matter of whether the men suitable for government ought to come from the family of Hāshim or from the family of Umayya or from any other group which was neither Hāshimite nor Umayyad in order that government might correctly be carried out and in order that the thrust of the conquests might steadily continue.

The matter was much more radical than such superficial suggestions. The view that a group could give up government and hand it over to another group would not save the situation. All that was really possible was that affairs should have been handed over to men specially chosen whom the Message had polished and imprinted with its character because the Message was the only thing which had been able to unite the various elements of the Arabian Peninsula in order to impel them forward in its determined strength. It was that determined strength which had been able to achieve the miracle of the conquests. If it had not been for the Message, the situation would have been the same as it was before. The sword of Khālid b. al-Walīd was the same as the one he had had in his hand before the Message. So why had it not been able earlier to conquer Iraq and destroy the government of Heraclius unless it was because of the Message, which had sharpened that sword, which had propelled that arm forward and which had created reason in the leader?

Muᶜāwiya, that clever man, was the same man who used to sprinkle dust on his forehead as he approached Hubal. He had not been able to see in a distant glance the lofty towers of Damascus with its green gardens and its splendour on the banks of the river Baradā until the Message had come. His resolution was derived from it. The lustre of his glory was taken from its magnificence so that there came to him the most powerful city whose roots were sunk in the heart of Greece.

Perhaps Saᶜd b. Abī Waqqāṣ would have only had a tent of skin and hair to resort to when his head used to rotate to seek the blessings of the goddess Manāt. If it had not been for the Message which he mounted in the bloom of his life of ignorance, he would not have dreamt that he would sit in the courtyard of Choesroe.

All of that was brought about by the wonderful action of the Message. There is no doubt that everything beyond it would bring the Arabs back to the situation in which they had been. This is in fact what occurred. ᶜUthmān b. ᶜAffān reverted to some of his old practices of the time of ignorance and deviated from some of the content of the Message. Similarly the Message, which he had been created to serve, came to be an awesome vacuum because of his use of men who did not understand it.

The Death of ᶜUthmān b. ᶜAffān

You would not have deserved to have been killed, old man . . . unless . . .

It is necessary at least that you should be credited with the virtue of preserving the blessed Qur'ān whose words you ordered to be collected and fixed between two covers to preserve it. That should have been enough to divert the arrowheads from your chest. Yet before you, the arrow of treachery had fixed itself in the breast of the one whom you succeeded. It was an arrow sharpened with every meaning. Yet it did not kill ʿUmar b. al-Khaṭṭāb in the same way as it killed you.

Fate has hidden forms in the blackest days . . . Among them is that which darts out on an arrowhead eaten by rust. Among them is that which glides between the narrow passes spitting out its poison with the kiss of a snake . . . Among them is that which keeps its talons and fangs hidden in the clothes of a sheep . . . Among them is that which twists among corners where hatred and malevolence putrify and the hands of virtue never touch them with generosity . . .

Storms of protest were raised against you but you pretended not to notice their arousal. When you woke up, the sword had anticipated reproach. The difference between you and ʿUmar b. al-Khaṭṭāb is that Abū Lu'lu'a rebelled against him because he wanted to protect the Arabian Peninsula from being mixed with foreign things which would lead to the corruption of its situation and would get in the way of its progress along its new policy. He fell dead as a result of his harsh attempt to view the future of his community as his opinion directed him. As for you, you were negligent by allowing room for poison to infiltrate into the fresh body of your state. That poison murdered you insofar as the mistakes of leadership were counted against you.

The First Revolution in the History of the Arabian Peninsula

The terror which settled over the scene – the shedding of the blood of the dead Caliph – was of the kind which follows the storm and which leaves clouds of dust in the air when it suddenly abates. The storm which raged and then abated was of the frenzied kind which blows in the desert without its power being lessened by the folds of the river-beds nor by the breasts of the hills. However, it was a revolution which blew in its gusts. The situation of the ruler in it had every power to set it in motion so that it raged at a time when he was the weakest man capable of withstanding it. This was the situation of ʿUthmān b. ʿAffān . . . He had been able to create the revolution or rather it had developed under him while he had sat on the throne of the caliphate but he was unable to withstand it.

The Arabian Peninsula had not experienced much in the way of revolutions in their true sense despite the fact that it had experienced them in their primitive forms. That was the attack which was its first teacher, at whose feet it was a student and it could only offer it in its meagre school some lessons in horsemanship. It mastered the art of drawing the sword and spear, of shooting the arrow, of mounting an animal, of saddling a camel and of swift galloping after game.

Islam came with its new Message. It brought about a revolution in circumstances. It was the first school which taught the Arabian Peninsula the art of impulses and the techniques of revolutions.

How sad it is for a nation which has not had a great school of such a noble kind!

Thus it was that the Arabian Peninsula began to feel the value of man in it. Islam was the dawn of its history. The rule of the third Caliph was the first examination for the students of the new school whose pillars had been planted in the great prophetic society. From the moment ʿUthmān b. ʿAffān took control of the government with that inner disposition which was fascinated by a love of arriving without this arriving having any but the most limited purposes, he was arranging things for himself without being aware of such a terrible end. When limited purposes are satisfied they restrict what is in them and the ruler is nothing but a consumer . . . Everything in life is like that. The means, which are employed to arrive at a result which is dispensed with immediately after it has been achieved, are not used to carry it out. Only in this way can the ruler be measured. If his goals are of the kind which lead nowhere, society will reject him when it has used up his use . . . Society has no mercy. Thus the means whose object is not attained are rejected just as the governor who harms what has been entrusted to him is rejected.

All of that was involved in the case of ʿUthmān. The revolution, whose opening the Message encompassed, came to reject selfishness because selfishness was a root cause for the formation of the elements of its impulses. Here it is the preoccupation with government and its spoils including treasures, amusement and enjoyment, which poured all their abundance on ʿUthmān and all the members of the family of Umayya, who circled under ʿUthmān, one relative after another. It was as if the conquest and all their gains were only to fill this vacuum and for the benefit of the family of Umayya themselves.

As stated earlier, the existence of the leaders of the family of Umayya would not strictly speaking have been the embodiment of mistakes if these men had followed a clear path of great purposes which were in harmony with the lines of the Message which had made all those purposes clear.

These are some of the direct causes for the creation of the revolution but they are not all of them. There are other indirect causes which led to these results. If you were to trace them back to their roots, the most appropriate of them is the six-fold meeting of election which chose him through the final delegation of ᶜAbd al-Raḥmān b. ᶜAwf.

In this respect it is necessary to study the situation in the Arabian Peninsula in a general way because there was an all-embracing understanding of the most appropriate leadership, which is well worth paying attention to.

It is well and clearly known that the Arabian Peninsula had, until the action of the new Message, been inhabited by a number of different societies within the one large society. Refractory tribes used to behave in ignorant ways. The history of Arabian Peninsula was littered with this primitive reality. A situation like this is equivalent to a general decline in society so that it will be reflected in its economy, in its thought and its communal life.

The Message came and was able, after fierce attempts to suppress it, to impose its new system. The Arabian Peninsula quickly accepted it because it found in it the right medicine to heal its illnesses. It should be clearly understood that the Message was a rationality and a philosophy which was in accord with the situation of the Arabian Peninsula. If it had not been that, society would not have accepted it so easily. However, in terms of being a rationality and philosophy it was also a reality which could only be realised in its activity because social man rejects philosophising rationality as knowledge and accepts it as influence and result, just as the sick man accepts the medicine only because of its benefit and not because of understanding its scientific composition. Such an understanding is shared by a small group called the élite. It is they who reflect this concept in the currents of society so that its true activity may take place. This élite is responsible to the extent of their understanding and they reflect what they understand. The highest leadership, then, should ultimately come from among these élite so that the appointment will be narrowed until it is limited to the summit of men.

The appointment may be wrong and it may be right. If it is right, that is the desired purpose. If it is wrong, then the results will equal the extent of the mistake. The result with regard to ᶜUthmān b. ᶜAffān points to the existence of errors. From that it can be understood that such leadership is the last point in a chain of election which is not correct. Otherwise he would be in harmony with the situation for which he was elected. The situation was the result of an intellectual revolution which had begun to discard the spirit of tribalism in order to put in its place the true leadership of society.

The Arabian Peninsula was convinced of the correctness of this principle and through it it had awoken to the true value of man. Therefore, it did not accept ᶜUthmān b. ᶜAffān as a dominating authority who would bring it back to its past, especially as its ulcerous past was not far away and was still connected with its present time.

The Message which had come to deal with the present situation in the Arabian Peninsula also had to deal with another situation in order to complete its purpose. That was the extension of the understanding of it so that it could extend the understanding of it from the élite to the general masses, so that the conviction of the truth of its method of dealing with situations might go beyond the feeling of its value to the profound feeling of the inner reality of this value. This is what brings it from the area of superficial knowledge to the area of the culture which acquires a great range by means of rational practice.

In the same way the conquests, which the state achieved after the call of the Message, had gathered its forces, began to reduce the cultural training which society was in need of as intellectual spiritual equipment with which to arm itself before arming itself with sword and spear. In this connection, it was essential that the election meeting should deal with this new situation in the light of reasoning which was appropriate for dealing with the situation of states, not by means of superficial bargains and by giving satisfaction to the spirit of past times.

The appointment of ᶜUthmān b. ᶜAffān to the caliphate did not take into consideration the senility of the man in terms of his inability to carry out any such real achievement and renewal. In the same way the problem had not been studied with the care which the seriousness of events demanded so that the cause continued to grow and increase until it exploded in a revolution which lead to the death of the man and which threw the new society into the jaws of internal revolutions. He began to deal with it as if there was a way-out whose advantage would be felt whenever need required him to complain publicly about a situation whether he had a right to make such a complaint or not.

The Situation Exposed

The situation which was exposed by the death of the Caliph could not have been covered by any of the other rivals. The experiment, which had been going on for a dozen years or so, was hardly capable of creating positive thinking about the nature of government and the need for responsibilities to be taken by mature leaders. That does not mean that maturity had become an all-embracing factor.

The hostile elements were divided into two groups: a group of leaders who aspired to pleasant positions and a group of people who complained of oppression and arbitrary government. However, the popular grievance did not have much influence with those leaders. It was only the gathering of injustice which clung to it through the corruption of the government.

It embarked on its action and then began to look for someone to fill the vacuum. There was present in their minds that leader who was capable of administering justice. He was the same man whom the situation had urgently needed for quarter of a century. At that tremendous moment that question came back which burned to find an answer: Why from the beginning had he been put aside from the situation for which he was the most appropriate?

The past had provided a veil by preventing insistence on looking for the answer. The present had no way to provide that veil. The position was one in which there was the greatest need to demand the answer.

ᶜAlī b. Abī Ṭālib was the very support of the basis of the community. In relation to the Message he was the whole Message, in its foundation, in the method of preserving it, in spreading it, in the ways of defending it. He had the greatest chain of noble qualities with which he was adorned. He was power, will, bravery, heroism, reason, knowledge, truth, justice, an exemplary model and perfection.

What prevented the reins of power being handed to a noble hand like this noble hand whose equal was not to be found in the whole of the Arabian Peninsula?

As for Abū ᶜUbayda b. Jarrāḥ, the present times refuse absolutely to listen to his advice. ᶜAlī b. Abī Ṭālib was not at any time in his youth less wise, less rightly guided, than he was at any time in his maturity. He was always anxious for the Message. He was noble and he gave complete satisfaction in his character and his qualities.

If he had accepted that the caliphate should go to some one else of the middle-aged leaders, it was because he was putting on the garment of self-denial. It was sufficient for him to see the Message reclaim the Arabian Peninsula from its ignorance to reason, from shame to pride, from the world to God, from stagnation to movement. In all that he tried to guide the steps of those who had preceded him to the leadership that was his right, being satisfied with the truth of his religion and its success. This was sufficient of the world for him.

As for the present, the Message had not remained in the same position and time. It had become widespread in extent and it could no longer be left in an exposed situation in which greedy men played around with it and competitors for power hurled it back and forth at one another. Let the bodies of Quraysh shake with fear. Let their machination stick in their throats. The valuable treasure will never be a target for plunder.

Thus was the resolution on the night of the death of the Caliph. Thus did the ear of the revolutionaries listen to hear the answer which they had continued to press to hear for quarter of a century from ᶜAlī b. Abī Ṭālib, himself.

Between Hesitation and Acceptance

They said to ᶜAlī: "We do not find today anyone with more right to this affair than you."

ᶜAlī replied: "Do not do it. I will be a better helper for you than leader."

In his speech on the day that they pledged allegiance to him, he said: "I am reluctant to take command of you unless I may be given full authority over you . . ."

The reason which made ᶜAlī b. Abī Ṭālib hesitate to accept the new caliphate was the same reason which made him accept it.

On one side, his own penetrating reason did not want the roles of such a tragedy to be played around the throne of leadership because that would be something which would lessen the value of the great position which had become a base for the greatest empire in the Arab East.

It was not to the advantage of this great expansion in the name of the new Message that it should become spread over the world that petty disputes about the way to arrive at the seat of power should gnaw at the custodians of the principles of its foundation instead of it being surrounded by conditions of greatness and respect, by which meagre petty whims were overcome much more than it should be characterised by a love of preference for greed . . . Because of that he strove to his utmost to prevent the bringing about the sight of such tragedy. He was striving to bury the revolution by diverting it through reform.

He would have been successful if Marwān b. al-Ḥakam had given him support in that, or if good intention had even brought the latter close to that . . . However, what occurred changed the means of assessment and changed the atmosphere into the darkness which was at its roots.

On another side, a new event came to focus all its lights on him. It was as if the revolution was looking at him before it began to move. It was a result of a consciousness of it and also of a lack of consciousness . . . It had decided and acted because ᶜAlī b. Abī Ṭālib filled its mind with all his greatness and his power. If he had not existed, it would have been less impelled to realise what it had embarked upon. However, the revolution was looking at him without listening to his wisdom and his advice. At all events, the revolution did not believe much in wisdom and advice.

In the face of this event, ᶜAlī b. Abī Ṭālib stood assessing affairs with disdain. He hesitated to accept the caliphate which was offered him as a duty because it came by a means in which there was a humiliation of leadership and a belittling of it, while it was something which should have been surrounded with protection and honour.

However, reality imposed another duty on him which left him without his firm disdain. An empty position is not something which can be disdained . . . Then he realised that those who aspired to an alluring position were the very people who were depriving it of its great awe and were now rushing to plunder it of what respect remained to it. It was not possible for him to be tempted by leadership. At no time did he ever seek the praise and treasures of the world. As much as was offered him, so much he rejected. However, he was compelled to seek the caliphate because he had complete faith in himself and there was no such faith in anyone else and by virtue of the fact that he was the one capable of defending the most blessed and noble task which thought set forth for the creation of the great man who was the inheritance of precious life.

He was no less concerned than the Prophet in the Message which the Prophet had put forward. He and the Prophet were its fathers. In these terms, the Apostle had said to him: "You, ᶜAlī, and I are the fathers of this community."

The Message belonged to him and it was part of him, of his reason, of his heart, and of his whole existence. So who could have more right to defend himself than him, himself?

Thus, it was not love of public appearance which impelled him earlier to demand this right. Nor was it love of acquisition of booty which now impelled him to accept . . . Indeed the Message, which had become a realisation of the objects for which it was built and which would never leave the Message, made him withdraw from anything less than its full extent.

ᶜAlī b. Abī Ṭālib answered the call of the revolution and accepted the caliphate. In his hands was equipment made ready for the government whose horizons had become overcast with gloom.

The Perfect Equipment

It is clear that the coming of the caliphate to ᶜAlī b. Abī Ṭālib was an unexpected occurrence . . . That was in relation to the events of the hour because it was not much expected that the rule of the third Caliph would end in him being killed, even though that had come to be something which should be taken into account during the last period of his reign.

Yet in relation to the new Caliph, the suddeness of government did not come upon someone without proper preparation for government. From the time of the death of the Apostle, even during the Prophet's own life and from the time of the announcement of the Message to the ruling assembly of Quraysh, he had been practising the administration of government. He had practised it while he was a youth watching over the movement of every change towards the noble Prophet. Then he had practised it while he was a young man who did not leave the company of his cousin for a moment while the latter was receiving inspiration and moulding it into clear verses. Then he had practised it while, in constant friendly association, the two held secret advisory meetings about how to transfer what had been given in trust into the framework of action. Then he had practised it in co-ordinating a protective emigration whose preparation and defence would give the Message time. Then he had practiced it on his return to Medina where the gatherings of the Anṣār waited for him.

Then he had practised it through his great faith and reason which produced in his tongue and his arms that rare bravery and heroism. He waded through the dust of a continuous sequence of glorious battles of defence in order to plant the Message on a basis of strength and firmness, which would make it rely upon them in the greatest and most wonderful outburst which the Message achieved on the pages of history.

As for the fact that he had been absent from the meeting in the hall of the Bann Sā'ida, that meeting in which his right to the caliphate had been abused, that did not prevent him from perfecting his practice of government throughout a quarter of a century. He continued to practise it by careful supervision and he went with it from event to event, participating with the three custodians of it with loyal sincerity as he was the first of the family of the Prophet, as he was the Companion of the Message, the first of the Companions, the most truthful of the reporters of the Traditions of the Prophet and the leaders of scholars of religious law. He was the man with the sincerest judgement and the most deep-rooted scholar of the time.

His practice of supervision was one of the most intense forms of training which he acquired. His skill extended from the correct administration of the people of the Arabian Peninsula to the correct administration of the rest of the peoples and the transference of the Message from its Meccan framework to its world role. How then could it be said that the caliphate did not come to ᶜAlī while he was in need of acquiring the proper administrative equipment for it? Rather the contrary – it galloped speedily to catch him up so that its path might be made straight by his path. Indeed his equipment to govern was ready and perfect . . . ready from its very basis with all the attributes of government.

These cannot be properly encompassed by many paragraphs of writing. From first to last they can only be limited and summarised within the structure of the personality.

It was only possible for ᶜAlī b. Abī Ṭālib to understand society as being a personality formed on the basis of virtues. He emphasised such virtues so that it would be possible to build from the structure of the Arabian Peninsula a structure which would gather its tribes into one tribe for the general benefit of the Arabian Peninsula. These alone, in his view, were the things which would build the true society.

It seems appropriate to illustrate this by drawing that heart like a tree under which man progresses in the lap of being, since he springs from it and to it he will return.

From the diagram opposite, it may be understood that being in its totality is God – the Mighty and Exalted – Who is the Great Cause. He is the complete essence, the perfect reality, the constant subsistence . . . unalterable and unchanged. Indeed an existence in which that which has no beginning and that which has no end come together. Out of being comes man with his two qualities: reason and body.

From the first aspect, reason which is unpolluted by the body is

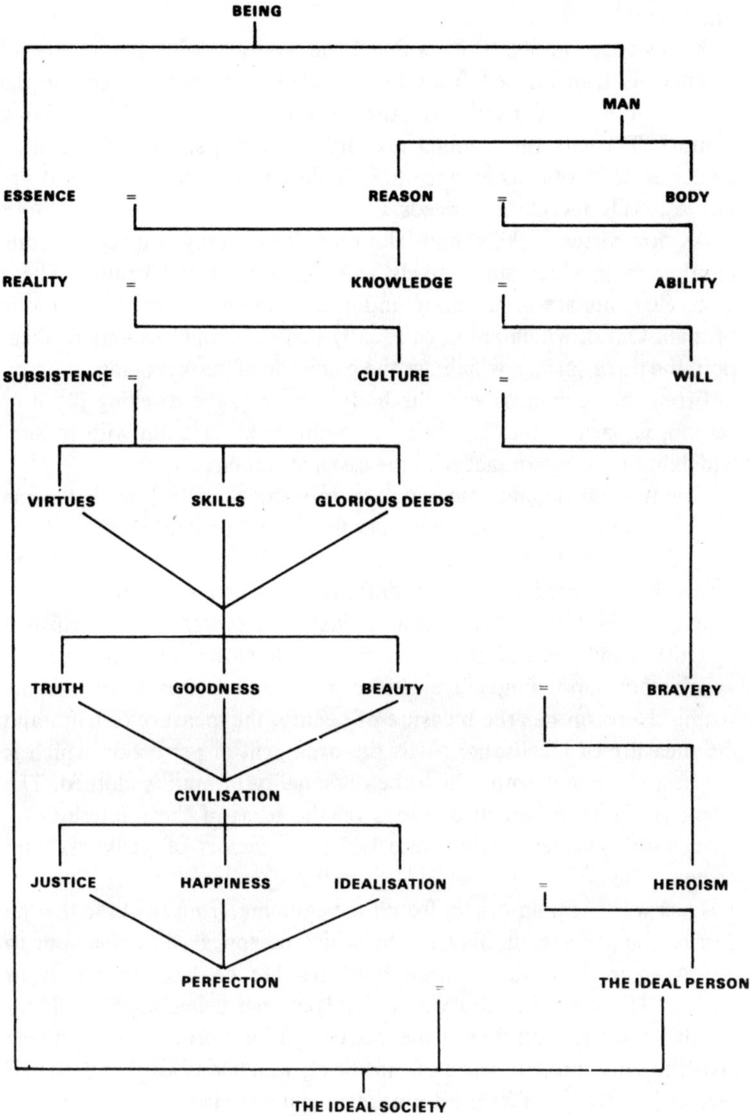
BEING
MAN
ESSENCE
=
REASON
=
BODY
REALITY
=
KNOWLEDGE
=
ABILITY
SUBSISTENCE
=
CULTURE
=
WILL
VIRTUES
SKILLS
GLORIOUS DEEDS
TRUTH
GOODNESS
BEAUTY
=
BRAVERY
CIVILISATION
JUSTICE
HAPPINESS
IDEALISATION
=
HEROISM
PERFECTION
=
THE IDEAL PERSON
THE IDEAL SOCIETY

paramount. This reason is what is able to come into contact with the essence of being so that from this contact it can beget the threads of knowledge.

Knowledge, in its turn, which is in contact with the reality of essence, is transformed from the metal of the soul to become the culture of man. Thus that culture is the result of this light-giving contact. Through this contact it coalesces and it subsists through its coalescence insofar as essence has singled it out. The results of it are virtues, skills and glorious deeds.

As for virtues, skills and glorious deeds, they impregnate one another to produce successively truth, goodness and beauty. These three elements are in harmony and in their lap grows the civilisations of man. Out of which are born equally justice, happiness and idealisation, the three springs which are the plenitude of perfect being.

From the second aspect, the body, which is the dwelling place of reason, is paramount. The body through its association with reason, which in turn is in contact with the essence, acquires ability.

Ability itself remains meaningless until the glory of knowledge has blessed it and at that time it becomes firmer and becomes will.

Will, in turn, lacks direction . . . Rich culture guides its steps and then will is adorned with the beautiful gleam which is bravery . . .

Bravery itself would remain an unjust force unless it was burnished by truth, goodness and beauty. Then it is transformed into heroism by which souls and minds live before arms and bodies have become strong. Heroism has the measure of beauty, the measure of truth and the measure of idealisation. It is the ornament of perfection which is the best ornament with which the personality of man is clothed. The result is a society which develops on the basis of these interlocking virtues into an ideal society into which no factors of weakness gain access.

Thus was the plan drawn from the beginning, from the time that he carried the Message in his hand by which he appeared as a saviour to the Arabian Peninsula. Throughout his life he had applied it to himself. His belief in God was a firmly-rooted belief so that seldom was his conversation free of the mention of his Lord. His reason was involved only in the essence of that being which was God and he had perfect knowledge of its most glorious meaning. He was trained in this knowledge of it because of an overflowing store of virtues and blessings so that it was only possible to say that ᶜAlī b. Abī Ṭālib was the ideal of magnanimity, truth and purity and the ideal of ability which was armed with faith, truth and justice. In him a firm will was enveloped and over him a rare bravery flowed. Through him an extraordinary heroism emanated so that his ideal personality stood out as the *exempla* for his people to build the Arabian Peninsula into that ideal structure.

Now he was constitutionally handed the control of the government, or rather the reins of government were thrust upon him as a result of the tremor born out of need for him.

Today's government is different from yesterday's. ᶜAlī b. Abī Ṭālib had had to bear the burdens of repair and the burdens of resumption along the last long journey. The Message was no longer a child crawling between Mecca and Medina. Now it had become that runner who covered vast distances regardless of borders. The swaddling clothes of childhood were no longer appropriate for it. It had come to need to gird its loins for its rapid journey. It did not descend upon any area without taking possession of its existing civilisation and its proved power. It would have been unjust that some who did not understand its value should have endeavoured to transmit its blazing glory.

ᶜAlī b. Abī Ṭālib understood that men who had not yet been completely enlightened by the Message were carrying it. The conquest which it had achieved had indeed been brought about by its actual power more than the power of those who carried it. When the conquest returned to his guidance, the result would only serve the wordly interest of the Arabian Peninsula to a slight extent. The Message, which was the world and religion, could not be absolutely confined within the borders of the Arabian Peninsula. Religion belonged to God and God did not only exist for the Arabian Peninsula.

In relation to the Message, the Arabian Peninsula had the pride of being its birthplace, the honour of being the place of its origin. How shameful for it to be less in value than its birthplace and lower in degree than what had issued from it. Because of that, ᶜAlī, in his concern for the Message and in his concern for the Arabian Peninsula, saw that the training of the inhabitants of the Arabian Peninsula in the virtues of the Message was the first duty which had to precede all the conquests. However, the conquests, in the name of the Message, had preceded the required order of progress. Instead of the hoped for benefit being achieved, they led to the contrary of that. The conquests which had been expected to strengthen and fortify the personality with virtue had brought it to a state where it became sunk in the midst of wealth and booty. These had corrupted with their world its religion in which its culture had not yet taken deep root.

Even so, the vicious whirlpool had struck ᶜUthmān b. ᶜAffān. So he built palaces at the expense of the sacred struggle and his family and friends sunk into the same squalor into which he had sunk, so that history records him with the mockery which sticks to his name and brings disgrace to the history of the conquests.

This present situation was no less urgently in need of being dealt with. Nor was a return to what had been before possible, nor was it possible to go forward with the old policy with the contents of its results. Thus the caliphate imposed on ᶜAlī the burden of struggling on two fronts: the front which involved treatment of the Arab personality again and a front which would deal with the conquests in order to restore their original meaning.

Here the chief problem was the leaders of the Arabian Peninsula who were still spurred on to go backwards to that pride in their tribalism which used to appear from time to time whenever occasions presented themselves to impel them into making their spirits, which were sick with love of leadership, take refuge in it. This was the case even to the extent that the kind of rule which had been ended with their relative and friend was no longer possible in the new mould which existed. Their preoccupation with expansion by conquest had helped them to remain like that insofar as they put themselves in charge of the waging of wars in order to increase their gain by that on the levels of materialism and power of leadership. The second level helped to realise the first. Thus they used the Message as a means and not as an end in itself. Every crisis which clashed with their interests made each of them jump to his tribe without showing any concern for the relapse which might affect the Message.

Another important problem, from another aspect, was the group of people, for whose sake the Message had come in order to alleviate their wretchedness and awaken the man that was in them. These people were the toys which those leaders still played with. They made them a vehicle for their whims and their caprices. They used them to attain their ends and the objects of their desire. Those very people, deprived of their culture, were hurled into the arena to bring about the conquests. The food of booty, at the hands of prisoners, brought them delight. However, even though that might continue for them for a day, it would never last for two days. The Message had only come to bring satisfaction to their whole lives and it would only ever bring real satisfaction to them by awakening their reason, the unique factor in the growth of their noble economy. Indeed the fruits of the conquest did bring satisfaction to all these people. Greedy hunger began to mobilise those who remained distant from the tables. Thus the Message which was created to unite was exposed once more to a disintegration which was even worse than what had existed before. It was amid such such chaos that the Arabian Peninsula was revolving in the last days of ᶜUthmān b. ᶜAffān so that when a revolution burst forth it could only have ᶜAlī b. Abī Ṭālib before its eyes as its saviour.

It was such kind of people in the Arabian Peninsula, from leaders who were always trying to strengthen their leadership to people who continued to be made wretched by what had affected them in their days of ignorance, it was this which faced ᶜAlī at the beginning of his Caliphate. So he had to look back to how he might build a new man who would be more appropriate as a properly developed instrument to bring to completion the true meaning of the conquests. In the face of this painful situation, ᶜAlī b. Abī Ṭālib buckled down to his difficult task of restoring and putting to use that heroism which had not become separated from him for a single day. It, its very self, had continued to be his equipment from the very moment he became aware of the Message until that day. There can be no help possible for anything which does not take refuge in it and in him it found the completion of all its conditions. It was for this reason that he was never content to allow any kind of bargaining and deals and why he would always use every one of his virtues without ever exhausting them in order to arrive at building a true man in the Arabian Peninsula. He would offer himself as the ideal model and he would give perfect support because he would remain the very titular head of faith in God, the idea of truth, magnanimity and sincerity, the ideal of bravery and heroism in the defence of the values of truth, goodness and beauty.

He would remain and along with him the noble Prophet, the two essential fathers of the Islamic Community.

III

THE BURDENS OF LEADERSHIP

ᶜAlī said: "Whoever sets himself up as an Imam over the people must begin by teaching himself before teaching the people. He will announce his training by his example before doing it by his tongue. The man who teaches and trains himself is more worthy of honour than the man who teaches and trains the people."

The New Standard

"We have come to a time when the most people have adopted treachery as something clever and when ignorant men have induced them into practising cunning plots . . . What is wrong with them?" Thus spoke ᶜAlī.

The new standard, which fluttered so preciously above the heads of the Muslims, which sheltered all the quarters of the Arabian Peninsula and under whose furl, conquest had spread from the rising of the sun in the East to its setting in the West, had become ragged in its threads and its colours had faded. It was no longer worthy, after quarter of a century, of realising the heart-beats of this passionate outburst and of shaking with this tempestuous power. Because of this, it was necessary to replace the standard of the eagle with another standard so that it could carry the true nature of the time and its flowing colour. Because of that, it was necessary that its threads be woven and its colours dyed in a way which would overcome time without disappearing or changing. This kind of firm weaving and thorough dyeing could only be found at that time in the shirt of ᶜUthmān.

Even up to the present time this shirt of ᶜUthmān is still the standard of throbbing bands of soldiers. No thread of it has yet become damp and the glow of its colours still remains. That is a painful reality . . . the shirt of ᶜUthmān. O, would that the Arabian Peninsula had never known a loom which wove such a shirt as this! Would that ᶜUthmān had never had any shirts! The Message had come to destroy such looms but destruction was his fate from them so that he was dressed in all the shirts from such looms.

Don't you see the practice of self sacrifice? Did not Jesus come before to destroy the wood of the cross? Yet was not the greatest of crosses his fate? And what of Socrates? Did he not take the cup in order to cleanse it from poison? But he could not do it until he had swallowed the poison. That is the story of ᶜAlī b. Abī Ṭālib during his age.

It was decreed that he should wear the shirt of ᶜUthmān. However, the shirt of ᶜUthmān did not have those solid threads nor did its colours have that glow. If ᶜAlī b. Abī Ṭālib had not put it on, it would have been put on in Demascus as evidence of crime. So generations saw it as always providing exoneration. Thus those who wore the shirt have put on the eternity of the crime and the shirt of ᶜUthmān remains for them the standard of the age.

The Beginning of Government

There is no doubt that the beginning of government was for ᶜAlī b. Abī Ṭālib a crowding in of burdens and the end would never be less than it. At all events, he did not seek government as a means of pleasure and enjoyment. Rather he sought it for its responsibilities and its burdens.

"The responsibility which has been put on men of knowledge is that they should not show approval of the gluttony of the wrongdoer, nor of starvation of the oppressed. They should not follow a path of reconciliation and softness towards that but they should firmly attack it."

Advice came to him from al-Maghīra b. Shuᶜba and Ibn ᶜAbbas that he should bargain and be friendly. He refused and said: "I will not cheat my religion. I will not give in to base conduct in my affairs."

How does he do that? Is his path unique and pure? Whom does he fear? What does he fear?

"Whoever fears death will not escape it. Whoever wants to remain here for ever will not be granted it."

Is it from the world that its treasures and bounties and praises are kept away from him? What can a man who has been created for the Next World do with this world? What will a man who will soon be deprived of wealth do with it while his responsibility and his account remain?

He did not wear things of the world except for a shirt of white cotton and respected armour. He did not eat except for a few grains of barley crushed in his hands, a dry morsel for his mouth. He did not live in palaces but rather in the humblest of huts. He did not ride any animals except a good horse in battle. For him poverty was an end, power a means.

"The world is a place in which I will come to end and its inhabitants will emigrate from it . . . It is pleasant in bloom. It comes quickly to the one who seeks it and it is obscure in the heart of the onlooker. Journey from it with the best of the provisions which are provided for you. Do not ask from it more than what is sufficient to live and do not seek from it more than the means of sustenance."

Once ʿĀsim b. Ziyād al-Ḥārithī asked him: "Commander of the faithful, why is your dress so rough and your food so coarse?"

"Woe upon you", he answered him, "I am not like you. God has required the Imams of justice to value themselves with the weakest of men so that the poor man is not disturbed by his poverty."

This world, which he dealt with ascetically and piously throughout his life and to which he stretched out his hand in honesty and truth and heroism, was something which he was never able at that time to grasp with the grasp of a beggar who loved it and of a man who was greedy for its apartments. He would never be a friend of it . . . At that time he only came forward to explain the programme of life which had been drawn up . . . how the world should be looked at; how it was possible to use it as a tool to arrive at the ultimate destination; how it was appropriate for man to act in it as a mature understanding reason; and how the protection of society could only be carried out on the basis of the consciousness of a rational person who was rightly guided.

Such a clear programme as this was the plan of ʿAlī b. Abī Ṭālib in all its facets. He laid it on himself and he lived it all his life. He spread it in all his words and actions . . . He was never able, in any way, in the world to reduce its value and to cut a single thread from the substance of its texture. He became, to the limit of himself, its constant colour and its ultimate support.

From this, bargaining was not a possible way to open its door. Nor did the threat of death have any real role in any part of his plan . . . because death, in his view, when it cut him off from life – and it would certainly do so – would never be able to cut him off from his Lord for Whom he worked and to Whom he would return.

He said: "I patched my cloak until I was ashamed of its patches. Someone asked me: Aren't you going to throw it away. I replied: Get away from me. In the morning the people will praise the generous Lord."

He also said just before his death: "Tomorrow you will look back at my time and my innermost thoughts will be revealed to you. You will recognise me after I have left my position and another has taken my place."

As he looked at ᶜUthmān following a plan which had not been drawn up by the Message, it became impossible for him, while he held the reins of government, to abandon the plan as it had been first laid out. Similarly the revolution which blew, rooting out corruption, would not have been born if it had not been for the fact that it drank from his wholesome spring.

Since bargaining was excluded in word and spirit from the speech of ᶜAlī, another word to express its meaning had to take its place . . . and it was firmness.

This firmness was not able to convey any frivolity. He had hewn it from that harshness with which the metals of truth and justice are adorned. He had coloured it with that magnamity and honesty and he had given it that bravery and heroism. Indeed it was a true expression of his absolute purity, his great preciousness, his thoughts of genius. He would never be without this firmness because it was the support of his unique personality. It was his guide throughout all his life. It is that which accompanied him in all his struggles and it is that which still accompanies him even now in the history of his eternal memory.

He began to carry out the administration at the moment in which he was handed the legal power of administration. He dismissed the governors whom the late Caliph had appointed over the territories, all conquered by the force of the Message. Instead of them he put men tested in virtue and he gave them a new slogan "cleanliness".

This cleanliness would be understood by such words as truth, honesty, sincerity, piety and kindness.

He never entrusted a governor with a task over the people without addressing such words as follows:-

"To Ashᶜath b. Qays, Governor of Azerbaijan,

Your task is not a means of fulfilling your appetite. Rather it is a trust invested in you. You will observe those who are above you. You have no right to offend your subjects. You will only risk trust. In your hands is wealth which is part of the wealth of God, the Mighty and High. You are only its storekeeper until you hand it over to me. Perhaps I may not be the worst of your rulers to you. Greetings".

"To Ziyad, son of his father,

I swear a true oath before God: If I am informed that you have betrayed any of the Muslims' booty, whether little or large, I will attack you with a violence which will leave you little wealth, a heavy back and meagre affairs. Greetings."

He also said to him: "Be a moderate man and leave off squandering. Remember tomorrow during today. Take from wealth the amount you need and offer the excess to the time of your need. Do you expect God to give you the reward of the believer while you are one of the proud towards Him? Do you aspire to Him while you wallow in pleasure? The weak and the widow will deny to Him that you should receive the reward of those who give alms. A man will only be rewarded for what he has done before and he will only reach what he set out to reach. Greetings."

In this manner did Imam ᶜAlī hand over the reins of affair to men on whom he imposed clean hands from his own hand and an honest programme from his own tongue and resolute actions from his own firmness. He distributed to them a list of the principles which it was necessary to adopt to block errors . . . .

"By God, if you found him whom women marry and by whom maindservants are owned, you would reject him."

"There is wide scope in justice . . . Whoever justice restricts would be even more restricted by injustice."

"A man who has no manhood has no religion."

"The liar has no honour.

"A branch of anything must grow out of its root."

"The shadow of the lame is crooked."

"The false circulates for an hour while the truth circulates until the Final Hour."

"Let not ambition tempt you and then God will make you free."

"Be a helper to the oppressed and an opponent to the oppressor."

"The poverty of leaders is easier than the leadership of the ignorant."

"At the final testing a man will be honoured or humiliated."

"A man's state is decided by his avoidance of things forbidden and his practice of things which are virtuous."

"The wickedest of rulers is the one feared by the innocent."

"The administration of justice involves three things: compassion with determination; a thorough examination of justice; and bestowing benefit with purpose."

"Truth is a cutting sword."

"A just Imam is better than lands and camels."

"The garment of reason is the noblest of clothes."

"Be assiduous in doing work whose rewards will not disappear."

"The one who rides injustice will be overturned by his mount."

. . . And so the advice and proverbs which this list contains go on . . . and they refer to no other way to behave.

This very firmness is what he gave to his leaders and governors whom he directed to work for the general policy under its inspiration. He restored justice to its true place. The refinement of the man of the Arabian Peninsula was the appropriate refinement for mankind . . . His opponents seized on it in order by that to meet him with that triviality and futility. They took refuge in the discord which they created. They had a matchstick from the shirt of ᶜUthmān.

The Ominous Shirt

Woe upon you, Nuᶜmān b. Bashīr, you who bear the crime which you wandered around with, which you gave body to, which you blew poison into and which you spread like a disease!

You, carrier of the plague whose evil pestilence will infect you, your family, your loins, your tribe, every area of the Arabian Peninsula . . . Muᶜāwiya, ᶜAmr b. al-ᶜĀṣ, Syria so that it moves from there just like the conquest moved to Egypt and Africa, to Iraq and Khurāsān . . . from this day of yours to your tomorrow, to the generations who will follow your time and will record your shame fashioned by your ignominy.

What are you carrying under your arm? What cover do you wrap around the verses of your Book and the praises of your struggle? Where do your feet take you, you trumpet-carrier and castanet of the Arabs. Woe upon you, did you not realise that the one who carries evil is worse than the evil, that the one who carries discord is worse than the discord!

O wronged relative who stayed away . . . slow down! Did you not spring to what should have guided you rightly as you walked along the road to Syria. It is your period ignorance which taught you to bury people alive. Fellow, if it did not teach you to bury the great evil and to suffocate blind discord, didn't your new religion?

O standard bearer of the conquest, has not the window of generosity in faith and the splendour of rationality opened in your heart? Go gently on your road, Nuᶜmān b. Bashīr . . . do not hurry. The shirt of ᶜUthmān which you carry, together with the cut fingers of Nā'ila which you take, is only your own worn-out shirt. You were still wearing it before you were born . . . It is the fingers of your left hand which were cut because of your ignorance as a punishment for theft. Yet you still steal, even now, the virtue of your new religion which you have adopted in order to carry the discord which you spread wherever you go. Stay in your place . . . Do not go beyond the borders of the Arabian Peninsula. Dig a deep hole and throw your shirt into it and hide your hatred and your malevolence in it. Then go back to where you fled from. It is not appropriate for you to spread the blood whose responsibility is heavy. Its burden is from the time of ignorance. Its concealment would be one of the virtues of your religion. Be above such an act. The vengeance which you strive for will only lead you to grief and destruction. Heaven will never be attained by you inasmuch as heaven was ever calculated for you.

Come back to reason. The tribulation whose fire will break out is not in your interest, nor in the interest of your Arabian Peninsula, if you gather fuel for it in order to increase its conflagration . . . Rather on the contrary, quench it by the spring of your intelligence and abate its blazing through the abundance of your wisdom if you have understanding . . . Pour some solace on its instead of poison . . . Ladle out for it from forgetfulness something which will heal it, not something which will tear it open.

O one who calls out . . . O bearer of a new reason . . . O carrier of true thought . . . O conqueror of new territories in the name of the Message . . . O raider against ignorance whose fortresses you destroy . . . You hesitate and there is nothing in the echo except poison. Shame upon you that you return to your barrenness, destroy your religion, alarm your people and curdle the splendour of your praises.

Bury that shirt. For God's sake bury it. . . . Act from your heart, from your reason, from your sinews . . . and then go back to your people. Give balm to a wound which is bleeding. Abate a rancour which is full of vengeance. Reunite a unit which has been dismembered. Call out the Message. It is great. It is all-embracing. It brings oneness and unity.

Do you not see, Nuʿmān b. Bashīr, that you should think and act?

The Painful Situation

The crisis which burst forth with the death of ʿUthmān and began to spread his shirt beyond the Arabian Peninsula, beyond every part of the world which the standard of the new religion had reached, was not a newly originated crisis. It had been the crisis of the Arabian

Peninsula since man had been there. It was a crisis which had been with it just like its economic situation had been with it.

The meanness of its land reflected a meanness in its way of life and in all its areas of work and thought. Its affairs had continued to be dealt with from the narrow aspects of customs and traditions in which they were clothed for a long period of time to the extent that to modify them had become something of great difficulty.

It had become known that the new Message had come to proclaim a new man who would be able to take control of his situation and develop it. The first thing which had to be begun was the preparation of reason so that it could become an actual force in the creation of this development and in propelling it to improve the economic situation. This structure, which aimed first at thought, had succeeded to a great extent in creating a man who had begun to use his reason.

In fact, the religious tendency which took possession of the reason of the Arabian Peninsula, really made it a centre for a number of intellectual eruptions, which branched out to East and West and which brought about some victories.

However, the Arabian Peninsula, whose reason the religion had been able to bring into motion, had not yet been able to submit its culture to it because culture is a continuous practice and reflection in the minds of men over a very long period. That culture was like the return of a voice after it had been wandering around all the areas of the cave in which the call had been issued . . . that is, the culture, with which the individual in society was adorned, led him from that society after it had completely embraced him. The new culture of the Arabian Peninsula was of a special kind. It had not reached beyond a position which remembered a time which was not more than four decades away. It was still a culture clearly mixed with what had gone before. It was a culture in a state of transition. Insofar as it was needed to be a basis for an impulse to realise a rational economy by dependance on which it would maintain its motivation and continuation, it did not achieve anything much worth mentioning of this kind. Rather the contrary to that occurred . . . .

The conquests which the Arabian Peninsula achieved sank it into a superfluity of colonial prosperity insofar as they enabled it to taste luxury without hardship. This permitted wealth was at first distributed among the leaders and the rulers, then gradually to the soldiers . . . until opulent classes were created as innovations. Materialism ruled as a tyrant over the spirit. Indeed that materialism became a stumbling-block in the way of a success which would have interwoven souls and minds with the original culture which should have slowly taken its place in society, which in that way would have been supported by a firm generous true economy.

This urge for temporary acquisitions did not include all the individuals among the people . . . Those who were first to take the battlefield were the ones who returned with booty. Out of that was produced a new class consciousness which divided society, awakened in it feelings of mutual envy and spread chaos.

The activities of the conquests came to require much administration in the organisation of the army, in the organisation of the poll-tax and the booty, in the organisation of pay and then also in the organisation of ideas and their correct propagation unblemished by errors . . . alongside the organisation of the distribution of booty and wages to the people who had begun to expect an end to their poverty from the new acquisitions to a greater extent than their slender economy could have formerly allowed them to expect. With all that it was not possible for a young state, occupied on every front, to organise itself and produce justice and equity.

Out of that grew deprivation which caused differences to appear in a society which the earnestness of religion had not yet regulated into sound systems of application. Then those leaders and rulers, who sought to enjoy the pleasures of wealth, began to hold on to their positions as a way of acquiring more. They began to protect their positions with a variety of methods. They gathered around themselves supporters and followers.

That was a new tribalism which now an economy of a transitory kind supported so that other groupings of direct opposition arose out of those who were deprived. They could only find this in their old tribalism. They began to gather under the banners of tribalism and to take them with them wherever they went.

In Kūfa, for example, they were divided into two groupings. The Eastern division belonged to the Yemenis and the Western division belonged to the tribes of Nizār.

Thus, we see, successively, that the success of the Message which had been brought to build up man in thought and in the economy in the Arabian Peninsula had been brought into conflict with those obstacles which had to be removed before it could continue its advance.

That had escaped it while it was taking its first steps along the road with ᶜUmar b. al-Khaṭṭāb, who had only drawn some partial plans which were more concerned with the military aspect than they were concerned with the cultural and spiritual problem and with sound economic direction.

In reality, the Arabian Peninsula was, and still is, in need of a spirituality capable of controlling whims and of preventing the eyes of the inhabitants of the Arabian Peninsula being opened on civilisations which they are not suited to be swallowed up by; and of preventing them from infiltrating into it without spiritual and intellectual preparation to acquire what is good and reject what is bad.

ᶜUmar b. al-Khaṭṭāb looked within the society and he saw that the existence of foreign elements in the situation of the Arabian Peninsula was spreading confusion toward the new Message, So he ordered the removal of those elements. The Christians travelled from Najrān to Syria. The Jews travelled to Arīḥā. By way of preparing the Arabian Peninsula to be a basis for a religious republic with pure blood, he prevented marriage with foreigners. He restricted ownership of property outside the Arabian Peninsula and he imposed limitations on this ownership like the payment of tithes, for example. Then he looked at the circumstances of the soldiers and how they had become integrated during the operations of conquest with the conquered peoples in such a way that this integration brought about an evil effect. So he set up special military camps to which the soldiers were to go after the end of every battle.

Al-Jawābī and Ḥims were the bases for the army in Syria, ᶜAmwās and Tiberias in Jordan, Kūfa and Baṣra in Iraq . . . . In order to control all these military activities he set up the military registers. This was the first operation to organise the affairs of state, to control its income and to distribute its works.

Similarly the census came as a factor towards the completion of these organisational operations aimed at bringing a distribution of wealth to the Muslims in semi-compensation for their meagre and weak economy. In its planning the economy did not appear to have any direction which could fix it on a sound technical basis. It had been somewhat strengthened in relation to what had come into the state from the widespread conquest which it had achieved with extraordinary speed. However, real concern for it had been abandoned for the time being so that its plans for the development of reason were based on borrowing from the surrounding civilizations everything which was beautiful and new.

Those were the aims and plans of ʿUmar b. al-Khaṭṭāb which looked to the future from a scientific point of view. Do you think that he was right in all those techniques? Or do you think that something of this kind would never be able to attain a degree of perfection without proper administrative experience? That had happened at the beginning of the administration in a state which had begun to establish its existence for the first time in its history – and these were only some plans and not all of them, which ought to have been drawn with full understanding and care. Steps toward them ought to have been taken with complete sincerity and impartiality and they should have been studied completely realistically with great restraint. They should then have been adopted fully and applied with every care and consideration.

In the case of ʿUthmān b. ʿAffān, he did not look for a plan to build society with the really sincere care or vigilant application which were necessary. . . . The state was allowed to stray away from its true purposes. The great values of the Message began to be dissipated through the temptations of conquest. Conquest itself became an end and a means towards which the people raced insofar as the battle-fronts had become a crowded centre towards which the majority of the inhabitants of the Arabian Peninsula had journeyed.

As for the rational spiritual structure of society, it had been neglected as a result of the diversion caused by numerous temptations, including property, valuable treasures, prisoners, servants and money . . . and so on down the list of things acquired by plunder and spoil.

The wise people in the Arabian Peninsula became annoyed at this, as did those who were deprived. . . . Even the conquered territories which had been seized by the splendour of the Message began to become annoyed with those who had started to make it lawful for their lands to be expropriated. The evidence for this is the fact that the support for the revolution against ʿUthmān b. ʿAffān came from hundreds of men from Egypt who came to complain against the Caliph's failure to show integrity in government. This was at the beginning of the foundation of the new state. Yet there is no doubt that the firm basis was that which was relied upon in the construction of the vast edifice whose outline the new religion had put forward. The mistakes which had occurred should only be reckoned against the leadership, since it had failed to show concern for reinforcing the works of the foundation. These mistakes led to results whose gravity began to worry ʿAlī b. Abī Ṭālib from the moment the helm of government was handed over to him.

We have alluded to such a concern in a previous section of this book, just as we have indicated that ʿAlī b. Abī Ṭālib was always aware of the situation while, in the isolation forced on him, he watched the course of events. Now he assumed the reins of government and at his disposal were plans to put matters right, to compensate for what had gone wrong and to resume the operation of building a sound structure.

However, the situation had become much more difficult than the situation which had faced the Message in its first stages. . . . Then man could be gradually brought to awareness and was complaining of the burden of pagan leadership over him because it was the cause of his isolation and poverty. Now man had been awakened, prepared, and had begun to claim leadership as a means of gaining profit and continuing those profits.

Then man had been an innocent child. . . . Now man had become corrupted by sexual temptation. Then a primitive rationality had been easy to acquire. . . . Now rationality had become again a disease which it added to its earlier state. It required treatment for two shared sicknesses. Then the economy was central and customary. . . . Now the economy permitted things which were not fair. Then the culture which had just begun to take on a rapid structure. . . . Now the awareness of civilisations led to the adoption of these civilisations without any proper understanding, and the harm from them was greater than the benefit. Finally, the man who had brought the Message had still been present then to give proper supervision and convey his influence. . . . Now his absence from the scene revealed the weakness of the planning which ought to have been taken at the establishment of the foundation. [Here we should note that we have already clearly indicated that at the level of the Message the planning was not weak, because experience had brought it in direct contact with the Qur'ān which was what brought about the Message through inspiration from Heaven. Imam ʿAlī was someone whom the Message had formed at the hand of the Prophet, peace be on him and his family. *(Note inserted by the Committee.)*]

All that was something which would never be easy to confront and to work to restore its organisation. . . . The conquest had carried it a long way away and it was in need of constant support to preserve its level.

The school of men who ought to have been able to understand these things in order to educate the rulers and leaders to submit to the leadership of these qualities, was not able to acquire the necessary equipment. The army itself, which had become tantamount to the whole community, which had been called upon to undertake these conquests, was not the custodian of any intellectual and cultural value. It was an army which strove for acquisition far more than it strove to spread high ideals truly worthy of the people among the civilisations which had now been provided with a new garb. The leaders did not have effective control over it in view of the weakness of the organisation and the weakness of the leadership. Even the Arabian Peninsula did not improve its economy through the new acquisitions. On the contrary these new acquisitions made it enjoy imaginary wealth quickly consumed and leaving a worse effect than the former situation.

Thus the vicious materialistic trend which entered through the conquest clashed with the culture which had gradually began to crystallise in the operation of illuminating reason and the soul. It sent it back to instincts and desires which were a permanent cause of the destruction of flourishing civilisations. How much more did it enter into a civilisation which was still shackled by its primitive chains! The extent of the situation existing then brought together the problem in order to throw on the shoulders of ᶜAlī b. Abī Ṭālib the greatest and most extensive responsibility which the history of the Arabian Peninsula had ever known. Thus through that he was the unhappiest ruler to carry the burdens of an entire people from the moment that he became conscious of himself until his death.

The Skies over Kūfa and Syria

Al-Nuᶜmān b. Bashīr had not so much gone to Syria through the strength of his legs as he had gone there through the greed of tribal fanaticism which had begun to split the state into two halves. He did not so much carry a shirt stained with blood as he carried a mental attitude enmeshed in feelings of hatred. He did not so much bring a message full of verses of the new religion as he brought discord wallowing in deceit and trickery.

That tribal fanaticism between the family of Hāshim and the family of Umayya, which, during the period of ignorance, had been kept within its narrow traditional scope, had now become clothed in a broad garment which conferred on it the fictitious title of policy. . . .

Thus was it so wrongly described as if it was some kind of heroism. This tribal fanaticism could not wait for the shirt of ᶜUthmān before it was mumbling with discontent and sticking out the venomous tongue of the serpent. Tribal fanaticism had already clothed ᶜUthmān himself from the time it had put him on the throne of the caliphate. It would be able to cut out a thousand shirts like this shirt when the omens gave it an opportunity.

Therefore the task of al-Nuᶜman b. Bashīr was a mere formality which distracted the attention of naive people and behind which the clever leaders hid in order to raise storms to defend their own interests and desires. History is not able to ignore the fact that ᶜAlī b. Abī Ṭālib was as innocent of the shirt of ᶜUthmān as the wolf was of the shirt of Joseph. Nor is history able to ignore the fact that the brothers of Joseph were the ones who made false charges against the wolf with the shirt of Joseph. However, it was the world which clung to its domain and used every means to gain its objectives and at that time Syria was under the command of Muᶜāwiya and ᶜAmr b. al-ᶜĀṣ. They resorted to such means as these and it was all the same to them whether the man accused of responsibility for the death of ᶜUthmān was innocent or not. The opportunity of opening a front against him presented itself to them. Any way, the man from the family of Umayya was dead and they were the family who had a right to seek vengeance.

The skies of Syria were cloaked in that darkness which gives warning of the approaching storm. Public opinion in the new empire was divided into three groupings:

A group which owed its allegiance to Muᶜāwiya and Syria was the centre of its axis.

A group which was sympathetic to Imam ᶜAlī and its centre was in Kūfa.

A neutral group which was inactive through the influence of Saᶜd b. Abī Waqqāṣ, the conqueror of Iraq and the man who squatted in the courtyard of Choesroe.

Each group began to collect its weapons together.

Let us leave the sword for a little. . . . It is not the appropriate weapon. Even though it has the pronouncement of separation in the field of battle, it is not always able to convey the inner meaning of victory.

Before we apply ourselves to that discussion, let us get rid of the third group because it threw away its weapons and withdrew from the battle. It began to look at its course as if it was not part of the battle and the battle was not part of it. It fled from its responsibilities. Avoiding responsibilities does more harm than good . . . insofar as it is more guilty than innocent. So let us go on.

The First Group – Syria

Since man had existed in the Arabian Peninsula, Syria had been the destination of his emigrations from it in order that it might send him back to it over the undulations of the epochs as a man nurtured by another residence. . . . Thus during many generations there had occurred a firmly rooted interchange across these two lines which beat in the heart of the desert. They met together, they intermingled and they separated so that they produced two inter-related societies from one stock. Thus the relationship of blood and the relationship of spirit brought together two peoples in a brotherhood from one source.

That is something which facilitated the final meeting between the Arabian Peninsula and Syria so that they exchanged embraces in the shelter of the new Message and with one fist they crushed the neck of the foreigner who turned his back in flight as he uttered his last farewell. "Greetings, land of Syria. . . . What a bountiful land you will be to the enemy!"

Muᶜāwiya had heard that historical farewell when he was harrying the departing enemy with the support of ᶜAmr b. al-ᶜĀṣ, Khālid b. al-Walīd and Abū Ubayda b. Jarrāḥ. History could not believe at that time that a handful of Bedouin who wandered about the desert burnt by the noonday sun could achieve such a glorious achievement and could demolish the outlines of a flourishing civilisation which had occupied a central place in ancient history. Indeed . . . that could not have occurred if it had not been for the Message whose thunderous roar had been pronounced by the great Prophet. It had brought the name of the greatest unity and thus it had unified the Arabian Peninsula with all its disputes. It had brought it together out of the diversity of its tribes and it had poured them into one mould. Then it had embarked upon the achievement of miracles.

That was through one force, which was the force of the family of Hāshim and the family of Umayya, the force of the tribes of Yemen and the tribes of Nizār, the force of the tribes of Qaḥṭān and the tribes of ᶜAdnān. By that weapon which unified minds and hearts, the miraculous conquest was accomplished. It was accomplished by the action of faith and by everything which radiates from faith. The gleam of the sword was from that light and it was carried by a united Arab force.

As for the time we are speaking of what made Muᶜāwiya think of relying on an old misleading weapon? . . . What made him think of exchanging the glorious standard of the eagle for a shirt stained with a crime? Did he have any words of praise on the day he blew the trumpets of tribalism to make the family of Umayya envy the family of Hāshim? Did the new false conquests ahead of him make him lose his reason in the delirium of the true conquest and the real victory? How was it possible for a man who carried the Message by which the lords of Byzantium had been conquered not to be able to resist the paroxysms in his soul by which it would return to the darkness of an ugly past? Was it possible, after this great and glorious victory which the Message had accomplished through him along the whole Syrian coast and whose name is registered in one of the most glorious pages of history that he could go back and give it one of the shameful marks of the petty quarrels which can be described as nothing more than jostling for position.

Arguments, however full of justifications for him launching this dreadful struggle, will never be able to get rid of all the accusations which have clung to this struggle . . . the crime of violating the Message through the hand of division, of stultifying the glory of the conquest with the mockery of quarrels and of dividing the young empire into two feuding halves.

At any event . . . the shirt of ᶜUthmān had settled over the skies of Syria. Now it was ready to unsheath the sword . . . but it was a sword which had lost its brightness.

The Second Group – Kūfa

Now we turn to Kūfa, another of the places in which the Arabian Peninsula settled. O how often did it open itself to those ancient emigrations and absorb them with their Bedouin life and then send back there a rejuvenated man. This deep cohesion was not lost for a day despite the armies which time after time descended on Iraq from the East, urged on by the desires of the Persians. Like Syria, the relationship of blood and the relationship of spirit brought together two peoples in a brotherhood from one source.

By virtue of this kinship, Iraq welcomed Khālid b. al-Walīd and made it possible for Saᶜd b. Abī Waqqāṣ to reach the courtyard of Choesroe. All that was carried out through the miracle of that woof whose threads had been made firm by the love which radiated from the source of the Message. . . . because the man from the tribes of Yemen and the man from the tribes of Muḍar supported each other, shoulder to shoulder, in launching into the field of battle, constantly repeating one slogan . . . "God is the greatest. *Allahu akbar.*"

On the day when a Caliph would deviate from the Message, then there would be a cry for his blood so that the man from the tribes of Nizār would fight against a man from Yemen and the Hāshmite would fight against the Umayyad, so that internal battle would begin which would forget about kinship and was only concerned to tear at wounds. In that way, everything would go back four decades and the glories of the community would be spilled. It was as if the glory, whose shadows had stretched from the furthest shore of Africa to the distant reaches of India, had become the toy of a child or the distraction of a deluded man. It was as if the Message, which had brought about the greatest miracle, had become a mere gust of wind in the atmosphere and a passing shade in the blazing sun. It was as if Syria and Iraq had not travelled together for a single day along the same road; as if no time during the earlier fighting had united them; as if they were not sprung from the same proud loins; as if they had not enjoyed together for a single moment the intoxication of victory; and as if no gentle breeze had ever settled over the skies. It was as if the Arabian Peninsula had never dreamed of a spring gushing from it by which its thirsty evenings would be cooled. . . . So it began to lap, just like it had, in its old stagnant turbid waters.

Thus the two fronts – the Kūfan front and the Syrian front – stood preparing to advance against each other with swords. Would that such a thing had never happened in Islam!

ᶜĀ'isha

O mother of the faithful, it is not a chapter which seeks to tear at wounds that brings your name forward in this book as being associated with a battle in which the blood of your Muslim sons was shed! Perhaps, O great mother, it would have been one of the things which you could have been praised for, if opportunities had been given to you to ride in your litter back to the borders of the Arabian Peninsula, where the conquest had begun to gather in the fruits of victory in bunches which spread their flowers over the grave of your great departed husband. History which has given a great deal of respect to you, may forgive you for tarnishing the letters of your gentle name with mistakes. You are not one of those women who live on the sidelines of events. . . . You are the wife of the most momentous name in life, insofar as you have become a mother to the greatest number of descendants and you are still, O venerable mother. Everyone who submits to his Lord seeks comfort in your warm lap as a token of sonship. Now the gates of errors have opened over you.

The barefaced interference in a battle, which was the fiercest internal battle which the Arabian Peninsula had fought, was not able to make you take the attitude of a mother who suffers at the sight of her sons marching towards death. No. . . . Indeed, it was the opposite of that. . . . You were in the vanguard of those who incited them. You carried beneath your arm two of the leaders of Quraysh. You began to travel with them between Mecca and Medina and between Medina and Baṣra. You went up on platforms to urge followers around you and around the two men. Insofar as you made preparations for battle, you were answered by the reply of men who defied death.

It is no wonder that your loud voice and eloquent explanation, coming as they did from a person whose close relationship with the Prophet gave her a powerful influence and a true response, were great aids in the preparation for that battle. It was a preparation which swallowed up the blood of Muslims without quenching its thirst, which painfully stultified the power of the emerging state and which enticed it into facing a chain of internal excesses by which its foundations were weakened and which took away its dignity from it. Thus you were a principal cause, in what happened later, for the decline of its greatness, the dimunition of its glory and the transfer of the centre of command from it.

The meaning of that, O illustrious mother, is not that if you had not followed such a partisan course, you would have been certainly able to repair the rent between the two fronts struggling for the seat of government. However, if you had followed a course of this kind, there would have been great hope in all probability for a lessening of the growing ferocity and for a prevention of the widespread clash of forces. If only you had led the camel which you had mounted into the middle of the arena, looked down from your litter with your radiant face and said with all brevity: "O believers, I am your mother. This is my tongue, my wrist, my heart and my love. Make me a barrier between your disputes."

Lady, if only you had done that, perhaps you might have been able to change the course of events because then the onlooker would have been able to see, hear and understand. . . . In your eyes, he would have seen the rays of love. In your face, he would have seen the rays of love. In the beckoning of your wrist, he would have seen the rays of love. . . . He would have sought to gather them all together and hear in them the call of love. He would have turned them all over in his memory and from them he would have understood the meaning of love.

Sincerity has the power to radiate itself. It is more eloquently expressed in the eye than on the tongue. You were the most appropriate person to be an abundant source of that sincerity. You were the mother of the faithful. In you all wordly aims should be forgotten. Government should not be your aim, nor leadership your desire. Your greatest wish should have been that you could bring the Muslims together to your love just as the Message had brought them together to its tent. All the praise which you could be given was that you were the great companion of the great man. After his death, your concern should only have been contemplation and reflection and care for the glorious thing which had been left in front of you.

As for those who competed for the caliphate, they had no claims on you except to approach you as a mediator and for them to come back from their dispute to accept good advice and wise counsel. None of that you did. You were satisfied with trivial assistance . . . so that what happened, happened. How were you tempted to that? How did you consider it to be correct?

This is what history has gathered together to record on the margin of the page on which your name is set down as a matter of caution, insofar as it would have been better for that page if it had been empty.

Lines on Ṭalḥa and al-Zubayr

The importance of the story of Ṭalḥa and al-Zubayr is not so much concerned with their personalities as with the evil effect, whose black traces they were able to leave over the length and breadth of the Arabian Peninsula. These two men, who trumpeted forth their close bonds of companionship with the Apostle, had not been able to acquire more of the Message than a peacock could acquire with its small raised head and its long feathered tail. Like this, they continued to carry on the Bedouin way of life of the period of ignorance under the brocade of imagined feathers so that it beguiled them on every occasion. . . . It was a Bedouin way of life which tied them to the past and an aristocratic attitude which raised their noses high. In these old worn out clothes, they could enter the fortress from a hole in the wall to sit there and remain sitting there until the Battle of the Camel. Throughout their lives they had accompanied each other, sometimes helping each other and sometimes quarreling with each other just as two wolves might accompany each other after a prey. Whether it was the prey or the companion who fell, either would become the prey.

In such a way each of them was hoping for the caliphate for himself. It was all the same for each whether he had the necessary equipment for it or not. . . . It was as if the fact that each of them was from Quraysh gave them sufficient ability to carry the burdens of government. This attitude of theirs continued until each of them became familiar with the points of weakness in ᶜUthmān b. ᶜAffān, then they dedicated themselves to the attempt to overthrow him. However, the revolution whose fire they helped to fuel, did not direct its eyes to these two persons in such measure. Soon the revolution rushed forward to its true hero in order to hand him its reins. Like a wounded snake which rolls on its wound trying to bite it in case that will heal it, they rolled over on their wounds, gnawing at them in Mecca until they were able to beguile the mother of the faithful. . . . Then she proceeded to join their forces.

Beyond the horizons, where Syria was sleeping uneasily, the leash of Muᶜāwiya gently extended its touch to them so that it might clothe the bunch already gathered by giving them the hope of the pledge of allegiance and the arrival of one of them at the chamber of the caliphate. Thus a contradictory kind of heroism blew through them both.

"God creates for you what you do not understand."

There was success for the new apostasy which the camel of ᶜĀ'isha, called ᶜAskar, lead. It began to tempt thousands of Muslims until it settled in Baṣra. . . . Then one day it met its fate.

A Side Battle

It is confirmed that through the activities of conquest, which had extended over the course of time, the Arab leaders acquired experience in battle to such an extent that they came to be considered as the most outstanding men of war of that period.

Khālid b. al-Walīd, who lost the Battle of Mu'ta, the first of his attempts against Byzantium near the Dead Sea, benefited from that defeat of his so that he gained more and more benefit in driving back the forces of apostasy which had rebelled against Abū Bakr. He never again tasted the food of disappointment, neither in his attack on al-

Ḥīra which he stripped away from the Sāssānids, nor in his siege of Damascus which he attacked driving the Byzantines out of it so that he struck the decisive blow against them at the Battle of Yarmūk.

This military skill, which the Islamic conquest gave to its men and its leaders and which put Khālid b. al-Walīd in the front rank of leaders, was the same as Muᶜāwiya, Sharḥabīl and ᶜAmr b. al-ᶜĀṣ had acquired in their attacks, whether against Egypt and Africa or against Armenia and Azerbaijan. It was the same skill which Muᶜāwiya and ᶜAmr b. al-ᶜĀṣ now used.

Instead of continuing to add more wordly wisdom to what they had by handing over the conquest to the Imam and by consolidating them on a firmly balanced and settled basis, they withdrew it from the conquest in order to use it, with all its cunning, on a front which they decided to open against the new Caliph, using the pretext of vengeance for the death of ᶜUthmān.

Opening such a front in the Arabian Peninsula itself was one of the cleverest and most strategic plans because moving the battle to the land of the enemy produces the best results, since then it is the land of the enemy which will suffer the losses. Thus Muᶜāwiya was able to launch his ship in the land of the Arabian Peninsula, by using Ṭalḥa and al-Zubayr, raising the hopes of one of them for the caliphate and anticipating through that to overcome both parties. Perhaps after that he would find the most suitable opportunity to announce another tremor which would bring him to his ultimate purpose which he had not yet alluded to up to that time. At the same time, he would not have to expend any of his forces which he had made ready for a time when there would be no doubt that he would need them.

He succeeded in everything which he aimed . . . Ṭalḥa and al-Zubayr, because they were Companions of the Prophet, were able, with the assistance of ᶜĀ'isha, the mother of the faithful, to form the required front. They set out with ᶜAskar, the name of the camel of ᶜĀ'isha, leading their troops to where they clashed with the troops of Imam ᶜAlī near Baṣra, to where the adversaries of the Caliph failed. The two leaders of the battle, Ṭalḥa and al-Zubayr, were killed and ᶜĀ'isha, the mother of the faithful, was captured and sent back to her home with full respect – while she was truly regretful and sorry.

The Battle of the Camel

It has been said that the Battle of the Camel ended in one day and thus it has been described as the shortest battle in history. But the victims of it came to more than fifteen thousand . . . the greatest number which it was possible for a battle to consume in one day. This means that in the shortest time it is possible to count the number killed in each second which passed in order to encompass such a slaughter which is numbered in thousands. However, the Battle of the Camel refuses to be described by such a meagre description which limits it to "one day". It is still examined, even today, by the most extensive and comprehensive words which can be used about it in order to draw out the full circumstances which describe and define it.

How is that the case? It is a battle which was the culmination of numerous battles which preceded it. It still goes on until this very day even after fourteen centuries, without it being known for how long its destructive effect will continue throughout the land that is called the world of Islam.

It became ignorant itself – at least almost – of the history of its birth. Also it became ignorant of the time when it was in the throes of death. It is no longer able to fix the great number of its victims because the number which fell beneath the hoof of the camel is only the least number which can be counted insofar as involved in it is the number of those who fell before, let alone the number of those who fell after. It is impossible to count those who will fall in the future which may still carry the venom of its poison.

Yet it prides itself on being at the beginning of history because what preceded it has ceased to be taken into reckoning since the period of ignorance clothed it in lack of responsibility. Greetings to the Battle of the Camel which has earned itself the name of the mother of problems.

The Right of Primogeniture

The Battle of Ṣiffīn came forward with much protest against its sister when the latter had preceded it to the right of primogeniture.

It claimed that it was born on the arena before it and that it had fed it and trained it to move its feet, that it was the one which bent over it with much affection before it had dared to stand by itself, and it had provided the way for it to walk and had supervised it with the happiness of the she-camel as she watches her young camel crawl beneath her nose . . . so that when it comes to the end of the field, its discovery and its great success are attributed to her.

The fact is that the Battle of Ṣiffīn is true in its claims, since if it had not been for the Battle of Ṣiffīn, the daughter of the camel would not have been able to dare to make its cruel attempt. Merit goes back to

Ṣiffīn in everything which can be called setting the path and playing with danger. Indeed the right of the primogeniture goes back to it. . . . It is the first-born; it is the basis of training; it is the teacher who understands all the acts of the battle-fields; it is what bites into time and acquires for it the power of flogging and endurance to launch into dangers; it is the one which becomes experienced in the affairs of the world. . . . What has become more subtle than it? What has become more disruptive and what more devious than its plans? What has become more erect? In fact, it was it which pushed its small sister on to the exposed stage while it was far from supporting it and nurturing its steps.

However, the onlooker will refuse to give the daring child the first prize unless it is worthy or at least it has ingratiated itself. As for the Battle of Ṣiffīn, its right will never be encroached upon, since it will remain the big sister of the Battle of the Camel for as long as it continues to acquire the right of motherhood. It is indeed sister and mother at one and the same time.

Yet the Battle of the Camel will never lose the merit of acknowledging gratitude.

It declares: Ṣiffīn is my sister and my mother at one and the same time . . . my mother who died – while I was a child – after an incurable sickness which the skilled doctors, who went round it under the veils of the Kaʿba, could not heal. Then the limbs of Hubal were destroyed and they were not able to cure it. Similarly the eyes of al-Lāt, al-ʿUzzā and Manāt were gouged out without a medicine being discovered. In the same way the angels of death at Badr, Uḥud and Khaybar were unable to root out the terrible constriction which tightened in the throat of the mother who had become weak. . . . Finally she fell into the throes of death.

All that the Battle of the Camel will declare and it will realise that its sister, Ṣiffīn, was the one who was in charge of its education until it reached maturity. Now it, that is the daughter of the Camel, when it marries an aristocrat, it will never claim possession of the wealth of this rich husband who died on his wedding night. So the big sister will have the great share of it.

A Review

It is indeed painful that the Battle of the Camel and the Battle of Ṣiffīn should be described with sad derision. However, it is the outburst of pain at frustrated hope.

Where is that splendour which accompanied the Arabs throughout their campaigns of conquests when chaplets of laurel were entwined on their heads? Where are those leaders of the routed enemy who were driven from one fortress to another dragging their tails of defeat behind them? Where are Heraclius, Rustum and Muqawwas? Where are Sergius Theodorus and Yazdigard the third? Where were the Sāssānids and where were the heroes of Rome?

Were all these allowed to restore their flagging spirits and regather their broken unity after having witnessed the conquering advance which now rolled on to its sides submerging them in its own spears and swords? What strength would the Arabs have later to confront all the events which would gather against them with the return of the tide? How would they face them with amputated arms and shackled swords?

All those events would gather against them and they would have to pay the tribute of the defeated to them in humiliation. It is a tribute, which their desertion of the contents of their Message imposes upon them, which their deviation from the true aims of conquest imposes on them. . . . If they had been aware of the true aims of conquest, they would have first aimed at conquering the ignorance in their souls, at cleansing the filth of tribal fanaticism from them and the desires which led soul and reason astray and made them wallow in the mud.

The Message was nothing more than a clear conquest in the victory of reason over ignorance. It opened the window of goodness on to the soul. It gave mutual tolerance in exchange for rancour, love in exchange for hate and it illuminated the world with religion. The battles of the Camel and Ṣiffīn could not answer the Message with any of its inspiration.

The Arab tribes of Yemen and Qays were the same ones still in the field and they were the same ones who still carried the spirit of the period of ignorance among the Arabs of the South and the Arabs of the North. They still longed for Qaḥṭān and ᶜAdnān. They were the ones who preserved the policy by which they were divided into competitors, under the shade of the Message, for the divisions of the world and the enjoyment of its wealth.

Muᶜāwiya had sought help from the tribes of Yemen until they had brought him to the throne of Syria. Later Abū Muslim al-Khurāsānī would seek the help of the Yemeni Tribe of Azd to demolish the Umayyad throne and hand it over to the ᶜAbbāsids. He would be able to do this insofar as the Umayyad Caliph Marwān would never be able to resist the ᶜAbbāsid advance because he would be, of all things, preoccupied with the tribal disputes between the tribes of Qays and Yemen. It would not only be in the motherland but even in Spain, to which it would be transported with the conquest of Qays and Yemen. Thus the tribal spirit would be the spiritual nourishment for the dreadful deeds which history has recorded.

It was violent tribalism whose traces the Message had come to burn away, to wipe out and to eradicate, in order to purify the atmosphere for a sound society based on a true creed and faith, on reason and correctness, on cleanliness and justice, on love and brotherhood.

However, the battles of the Camel and Ṣiffīn only had the eyes of a camel whose concern was to feed on the pasture of a green oasis, no matter whether it would deplete the Tigris and Baradā, or whether the Euphrates would sink down.

Some words on Ṣiffīn

Just north of al-Raqqa on the Western bank of the Euphrates stands Ṣiffīn.

After numerous warnings and the failed attempts to avert this clash made by the messengers between the new Caliph and Muᶜāwiya, the advance to put down the rebellion was decided. The two mobilised armies met at Siffīn. Two weeks were spent in light skirmishes. The purpose of these for Muᶜāwiya was to lure the opposing army into desertion so that he would take over the affairs of the Muslims.

He did not succeed in the attempt.

Then Muᶜāwiya prevented the army of ᶜAlī from getting access to water. Thus the army of the Caliph could only drink by using force but it did not respond to its opponents with similar treatment. A cunning plan had been used to incite emotion but it had failed.

The two armies joined together in a fierce battle. The full circle of defeat was about to turn on the army of Syria. Muᶜāwiya sought the aid of ᶜAmr b. al-ᶜĀṣ to devise a ruse. ᶜAmr b. al-ᶜĀṣ thought of a good scheme and advised that copies of the Qur'ān be raised and that arbitration be sought.

After numerous deliberations, under pressure from some of the supporters, especially those who would be later called the Khārijites and in order to avoid further shedding of blood, the arbitration was accepted. However, the Imam was forced to accept it.

ᶜAmr b. al-ᶜĀṣ would represent Muᶜāwiya.

Abū Mūsā al-Ashᶜarī would represent ᶜAlī.

A mockery of history was carried out through the treachery of the arbitrator, Abū Mūsā al-Ashʿarī . . . insofar as he dismissed ʿAlī b. Abī Ṭālib from the caliphate. The outcome was tens of thousands killed.

The battle resumed. . . .

The unity of Islam was torn asunder. . . .

The Khārijites appeared. . . .

The conquest became atrophied. . . .

There was the assassination of the greatest man capable of defending the community and fixing it firmly on a basis of noble deeds and virtues, by whom it would be perfected for ever, if and when it acted.

A Result of Ṣiffīn

Since the fox has a right to be proud of his cunning, does any kind of guilt enter into this pride? Yet, the tail claims that the head which devised the cunning tricks has not gone once into its dangers without it having to go with it. . . . It is its companion in every step which is taken towards the realisation of its art of trickery.

Since the situation is like this, the Battle of Nahrawān has the undisputed right to claim that it is the long tail of the Battle of Ṣiffīn.

However, even though it was cut off by one blow, it did not pass without spreading around it signs of astonishment and distress beyond the tails which it left which are still dragged along even today, encompassing as they do philosophies which split from each other such as argumentative sophistries split away from quarrelsome contentions.

Yet, the Khārijites, in all their branches, Azaraqites, Najdites to Ibādites and Sufrites, including all their groups which had twenties – in their extremism or their justice, in their democracy or in their aristocracy – were entitled to some honour because they were searching for truth, however mistakenly. Thus the Imam said of them before his death: "Do not fight against the Khārijites after me. One who seeks truth and is mistaken is not the same as one who seeks falsehood and gains it " Similarly ʿUmar b. ʿAbd al-ʿAzīz said of them: "I know that you have not gone out of the community to seek for the world and pleasure. You want the Next World but you have mistaken the way to it."

The consequence of the Battle of Ṣiffīn was the Battle of Nahrawān. Its existence was sufficient misery for it. Beyond what it severed from the Islamic world at the dawn of its unity and the beginning of its glory, it caused the injection of the poison of rancour in the breast of one particular Khārijite. Then he gave his sword that poison to drink and set out to kill the greatest man after the Prophet whom the history of the Arabs has known.

The Haunches of Abū Mūsā al-Ashᶜarī

It is certain that you, Abū Mūsā, were not of that dough which, when baked, the tables long for. Nor was your wood from the plant whose light, when burnt, is pure and whose smoke is scent. Nor was your support of that daring kind which did not fear to expose itself to the critical test by which the purity of metal is made clear.

You were given the reins of Kūfa and your wood became twisted there just like a stick becomes twisted in the hand of a blind man.

What benefit does a blind man have from the guidance of one who is deceived? Therefore, Kūfa threw you out when it had delegated you to be the stick on which it should lean for support. It did not find anything more than a twisted form in you.

As for you, you remained squashed on your haunches which you puffed up with some juridical knowledge so that your flexible wood became better thought of. However, you did not hide your secrets from ᶜAlī b. Abī Ṭālib. He was the man who left you in command of Kūfa hoping to cleanse your nature there. He is the man who removed you after your wood became barbarianised. Yet the fates which are bound to every ridiculous event only felt it good to put you forward on the track towards the meeting place where all caravans meet.

Shame on your haunches puffed up with knowledge and scattered dust!

Aftermath

No sooner had the Battle of Nahrawān come to an end than the fighting between ᶜAlī and Muᶜāwiya returned to the state it had been in earlier. Sometimes it involved serious military attacks and at other times it was limited to skirmishes which had the character of trickery and cunning. Actions of chaos and destruction were developed in order to spread terror and destroy sleep.

As for the people whose nerves were tortured by all these kinds of terrible acts, they were the target of psychological disruption as a result of which they wavered between angry outbursts because of his kindness and the resumption of battle and between submission and loathing from a battle which would in any case make them the losers.

The continuation had become the very same thing. There

throughout the Syrian front was the Yemenis and here in the lines of Kūfa were the tribes of Qays. Between the tribes of Yemen and Qays there were threads, connected to the various different tribes and bound together either by marriage and kinship or by spiritual interest and selfishness. Anticipation was sharpened by any one of the two groups tipping the balance of support.

These were the considerations and balancing that had to be taken into account. The movement of people began to occur to join the camp where they could secure the satisfaction of their desires and demands.

It was not possible for those skirmishes to come to an end. They had become the present condition. Therefore a truce was made between the two warring factions, to which the two parties submitted. In it the administrative division was laid down in order to save blood and a disaster to a good name which had begun to turn yellow like the cheeks of a sick man turn yellow on his sick bed.

The Truce

Was it a truce or was it the gulping down of a policy which spread its total failure to every area of the Arab world, including the Arabian Peninsula, Syria, Yemen and Egypt? Was not that act a failure which lead Muᶜāwiya to let the conquest stagnate and to agree to pay tribute to Constantine the Second, the ruler of Byzantium? Was not that act a failure which required ᶜAlī b. Abī Ṭālib to withdraw his plans for actions of conquest on the Eastern front so that he let the quaking Persians return to the leadership of the daughter of Choesroe who proceeded to try to restore the glories of her father, which had become grieved by the conquest which had brought the Message in one hand and then begun to gather together prisoners, spoils and booty with the other hand.

Khālid b. Fāris, ᶜAlī's governor over Khurāsān, had been able to capture the quaking princess at Nisāpūr and he had led her under guard before the Caliph. . . . However, ᶜAlī b. Abī Ṭālib, who was a man incapable of finding pleasure in the ways in which conquests had been conducted since conquest had begun, did not treat the captive princess with the moral treatment which is given to prisoners of war. He gave her the opportunity of choosing the man she wanted and then he would marry her to him. However, she would only accept the man who had the right of precedence in the state. ᶜAlī, who was an illustrious man of middle age, disdained to accept a marriage which lacked the elements of harmony so that later the captive had complete freedom.

This is a small example, which ᶜAlī b. Abī Ṭālib gave, about the manner of conducting the conquests towards high goals. It was inappropriate that desires for acquisitions should sully them. Nor should the aims of plunder or desires for debased enjoyment alter their essence so that he controlled animal inclinations which incited blind sexual desires.

In those days, a marriage which was a kind of political acquisition to bind tribes with bonds of kinship in order to lessen tribal warfare . . . was not able to bring about the desired object. Thus the conquest continued to be exposed to decline into lusts and to be burnt in the inferno of desires, so that it was distracted from the current of high ideas and turned aside from the refuge of spiritual acquisitions.

ᶜAlī b. Abī Ṭālib, a man full of the nobilities of thought and sensitive to the passions of the spirit, was not capable of being content with the world which was dragging its tracks, stained with the sexual desire and animal passion, across the conquest. Whether or not he was able to impose that with the force of law, after the weight of events and their heedless disregard in bringing about true policies and in confining them within the great words of the Qur'ān and its swelling examples, the important task had now come to him of taking over its records which have been associated with his name and with the name of the great call for every generation which hands on the Message in order for it to be poured into moulds for its true programme.

He came to the view that the Arabian Peninsula, which had recorded the merit of spreading the great call, would not be completely able to take hold of its glory except like a shot takes hold of its echo as it is sent back. This he felt while Muᶜāwiya was making Syria his stronghold.

Material acquisitions, which come on the periphery, are only like the downpour of rain which the clouds bring over and then swallow up.

Let the truce be. . . . And with it let there be a submission to the cultural and psychological reality which has never been able to impose unity on the natures of the Arabs from the first moment at which they felt the delight of the taste of this unity, only in order to feel the disappointment of the division whose different layers presented shattering selfishness and only to shun, as their sick desires wanted them to shun, every ideal which had come to clear the thorns away from their path.

Let this child crawl by himself and likewise let him fall by himself. Let his crawling and falling be repeated along the road which is open before his feet. Every bruise on his knees will remind him of his turning aside from the main path.

[The practice of the tested apostolic Imam, blessing be upon him, demonstrates that he did not submit even at the final moment. Rather he continued to live a life of struggle for the sake of changing the situation until he was struck dead. There is evidence that he was preparing a wide military campaign against the front of deviation to limit the attacks. Nothing stopped him from implementing that except his death as a martyr in the house of his Lord. (*Note inserted by the Committee*)].

19th Ramaḍān

On this day ʿAbd al-Raḥmān b. Muljam made his appointment with heroic acts. He had decided to sharpen his sword and to sweeten it with a handful of poison so that he might kill ʿAlī b. Abī Ṭālib with it.

Quṭām, the beautiful alluring woman, had steadied his nerves. The father and brother of this Quṭām had taken part in all the battles but they had been killed at the Battle of Nahrawān and had gone to meet their Lord, leaving a heavy shade of hatred which still continues, even until today, to infiltrate beneath its doorway into souls sick with the disease of hatred and pride.

As for the bereft daughter, she would never sleep in the arms of her enthralled lover unless he gave her the head of ʿAlī b. Abī Ṭālib as a dowry. Thus did 19th Ramaḍān settle in history, insofar as the pages of history have been moved to remember it.

IV

TRANSITIONS

Nahj al-Balāgha

Some men have suggested that the hand which stretched towards composing *Nahj al-Balāgha* was a long distant hand which was longer than three centuries after ᶜAlī. This hand had only stretched to play with words and form them as the art of forgery wished.

If the case was like that, then the forger has the claim of being the greatest offender in the field of art. . . . He was able to study the period thoroughly and immerse himself in the spirituality of ᶜAlī b. Abī Ṭālib to a degree which entitles him to enter into it completely. He was outstanding in the art of direction, the art of administration, the art of reproduction, the art of representation. Even while he was imitating, he was appearing in the genuine form. The visitor has fused into the original and the intention is lost within.

What thing, which has been set down in *Nahj al-Balāgha*, was not a true portrayal of that personality which has been set down in the body of ᶜAlī b. Abī Ṭālib, just as the light of the sun comes down on the translucent cup? What action which ᶜAlī b. Abī Ṭālib accomplished during his life was not the ultimate expression of the truth of those high ideals with which his pure soul blazed? Indeed they abound in every one of his expressions, in every one of his suggestions and in the whole totality of his book.

What has come in *Nahj al-Balāgha* crushes any doubt about what has come in *Nahj al-Balāgha.*

Was this book not the assessment by the great man of his extensive programme of reform in which he cultivated for man a value which is crystallised in sound reasoning and which elevates virtue? Did it not cause virtue to grow and to revolve around one pivot, the pivot of piety and belief in God?

When, and at what moment in his life, did he not express this clear programme? Was ; in his proclamation of the Message and his belief in it, while he deaicated his himself to summoning men to it and fighting for its achievement? Or was it in its application as a perfect constitution for all the currents of his thought, his statements and his actions in terms of his asceticism, his bravery and his heroism?

Since *Nahj al-Balāgha* is crammed with expressions which carry such ideas as these which no heart could have poured forth as a mere attribution to him by using such words which could only have sprung from his pen, that accusation will never harm *Nahj al-Balāgha* in any way. Indeed the language involved has come down truthfully with a picture of himself as a model appropriate for the genuine ideas. Indeed the rhetoric, in its real conception, does not exist absolutely in the power of the language and description inasmuch as it is a revelation of high ideals in moulds which are firm in arrangement and texture.

Yet even these last would remain forever empty moulds as long as those charms were not perfected in them.

Whether the words of *Nahj al-Balāgha* were written by ᶜAlī b. Abī Ṭālib – and that is what is true – or whether it was written by some accomplished scholar, it preserves a permanent expression, profound in its rhetoric, of the psychology of one man called ᶜAlī b. Abī Ṭālib.

The Intelligent Arabs

It is said that the intelligent Arabs are four. Men divide intelligence between them. The right of first place is given to Muᶜāwiya b. Abī Sufyān since they grant him the power of deliberation and careful thought. They give ᶜAmr b. al-ᶜĀṣ the special characteristic of spontaneous improvisation in view of him being a master at putting forward contrived solutions when difficulties become severe and unexpected events are scattered around. On al-Mughīra b. Shuᶜba they bestow the ability to classify problems. They leave to Ziyād, the son of his father, the final classification of everything large or small.

The observer will notice that in this division, intelligence was the quality of the family Umayya, both in the person of Muᶜāwiya and those who wrapped themselves within his orbit insofar as no trace of it has been pointed to in what came before this period of history. . . . It is as if as a result of his acquisition there remains no right for the generations which follow to claim any association with it.

Does the observer also inquire in the case of Ziyād, the son of his father, about what time this noble gift was given to him? Was it when his inclination and favour were with ᶜAlī b. Abī Ṭālib or when Muᶜāwiya recognised a forgotten brotherhood with him and embraced him to his breast as the brother whom he had made a brother and whom he had given the reins of power over revolutionary Baṣra and recalcitrant Kūfa?

The observer will also not hesitate to show his surprise and bewilderment, when he sees that age divided into two warring halves, about how it is one half which has the entire share of intelligence since nothing remains with which to adorn the other half.

However, the intelligence which is intended is not the intelligence which scientific reality and philosophic thought recognise. In reality intelligence is a high degree of mental acumen by which reason acts with adroit execution towards all difficult problems which arise in the course of life demanding to be solved and dealt with. Since it is a test of the power of reason and the depth of its scope, it is at the same time, in the manner of its practice, an expression of the power of the soul and the extent of the purity in its essence. It will never have a noble situation unless it is a product which has combined a sound reason and a noble soul.

Indeed, in the conception of it which they put forward with these four men, it is nothing but a weapon which people of the world resort to in order to attain their aims. Those men whose souls are seized with the desire to abstain from the world do not have much need of it. It is a weapon whose ribs are built up on cheating and deceit much more than they are composed of truth and frankness. Therefore it is of more use, more influential in scope and a more flexible means for men of selfish interest than it is for men who have little interest in the world and its pleasure and its deceptive brightness.

This does not mean that the latter group of people do not have a mind which can serve as a pasture for the kind of game which is adorned with such qualities. However, they have too high an opinion of themselves to resort to techniques which are coloured by any kind of duplicity and deception. More than that, they have no need of the techniques of misrepresentation and trickery because they live with an unselfish attitude towards the world and they long for the Next World with honesty, truth and good hopes.

Yet it should not be understood that these ascetics absolutely rejected the world and did not give it any concern. Rather they intended, through severe testing in it, to lessen their approach to it from being like that of those hungry with greed so that mad rushing towards it should not be a way by which the essence of man would lose his beautiful ideals, the most radiant of which is honesty. A human society which falls into moral decline does so because of its failure to acquire the true values of living civilised societies.

Therefore this intelligence was a weapon of the world in the battle which was taking place between ᶜAlī b. Abī Ṭālib on the one side and Muᶜāwiya b. Abī Sufyān on the other. Muᶜāwiya obeyed this intelligence and it was a flexible tool in his hands. In reality, he was entitled to claim deliberation and careful consideration which is the first and most outstanding of the qualities of intelligence, its most profound and its calmest ornament of the intellect. But he acted with it like the people of the world and he did not act with it like those who are not deceived by the pleasures of the world and the glitter of their imaginations.

Deliberation, in its true sense, is only to look into affairs and to examine their consequence profoundly and to grasp them with the most distant view which it is possible to take. At this point there is a great difference between the deliberation which a pious man uses and the deliberation which a man of the world uses. The latter looks at the earth with earthly eyes and sees nothing beyond the earth. The former, on the other hand, looks at the earth as a base form from which he may jump to a far destination which ridicules distances and scoffs at borders because it beholds existence from its particles to its totality and sees that the journey along the long path will only ever be with each secure step.

After Muᶜāwiya deliberated, he acted. . . . After ᶜAlī deliberated, he acted. The deliberation of Muᶜāwiya was correct and attained power for time. The deliberation of ᶜAlī was correct and he took possession of time.

Muᶜāwiya had used deliberation for conquests and deliberation responded to him and dazzled him with conquests. He embraced the practice. Kingship became one of his distant aims and he would arrive at it one day with all the accesses, entrances and exits which deliberation provided for him without avoiding sin and with no disapproval. However, no sooner had the conquest of Syria been completed than he began to make a base for himself in it. He determined to rely upon it as the support of his future. He began to anticipate chance happenings and sudden events. Deliberation guided him to the sure way to carry out his plans. Generosity was the first of the ways which he set down to gain the hearts of his supporters. Many were those who were not deprived of this material attachment by which he gained power over them and with which he led them on his leash.

Maymūn b. Mihrān has said: "Muᶜāwiya was the first one who raised the military salary to two thousand dirhams."

However, the caliphate, by virtue of its nature, was for the man who was most appropriate for it. There was no way to it for Muᶜāwiya while the Emigrants, the aged men, the Companions and the relatives of the Prophet were men with priority in Islam and great merit. Yet Muʿāwiya, believing in generosity at appropriate times and the surprises caused by sudden events, did not cut the thread of hope which he had for it . . . especially as he was well-known for his lenient gentle feelings.

When ʿUmar b. al-Khaṭṭāb was killed, he panted to help ʿUthman b. ʿAffān with all his power to attain the Caliphate. Then the thorn of his cruelty became stronger and the wood of his nature became harder.

ʿUthmān was an old man whose life would not last long. Here was a new hope which extended its threads to the caliphate with the end of the caliphate of ʿUthmān.

As ʿAmr b. al-ʿĀṣ, he abandoned the activities of conquest. He had suffered hardships and risked dangers until he had achieved the conquest of Egypt and taken control of it so that he might move from there to achieve an aim whose true intent he kept hidden from Muʿāwiya.

ʿUthmān dismissed ʿAmr b. al-ʿĀṣ and put his own brother-in-nurture, ʿAbd Allāh b. Abī Sarḥ, in his place. Muʿāwiya did not get angry at this change. It was part of the plan drawn up in his imagination to reduce the number of competitors.

The revolution against ʿUthmān b. ʿAffān, which led to his death, did not come as a startling surprise to Muʿāwiya, even though he contrived the appearance of great grief.

When he received the shirt of ʿUthmān and hung it up in Syria in order to excite men's emotions and when he used Sharḥabīl b. al-Ṣimṭ to go round telling of the effects of the crime to all the Syrians in order to call upon them to take vengeance . . . all that was part of the execution of the plan drawn up to get to the desired throne.

Many were the plans which this deliberation drew up for him along the road to the throne of Syria. All of them were precise in their application and precise in their execution. They included actions from the opening of the campaign against his rival in the Ḥijāz under the leadership of Ṭalḥa and al-Zubayr to the concoction of destructive incidents under the leadership of al-Ḍaḥḥāk b. Qays, to the Battle of Ṣiffīn and the raising of copies of the Qur'ān, to the treachery of the arbitration, to the supervision of the Battle of Nahrawān and the confidence of its good results being in the service of his interests and of the success of his plans, to the deliberate sinking of the ship of Qays b. Saʿd b. ʿUbāda, the governor of Egypt and a man who represented ʿAlī with clean hands and good administration and surpassed Muʿāwiya in rational deliberative intelligence. As a result of the latter action the man was kept away from his post and Muḥammad b. Abī Bakr took his place. He worked to try to overcome the inhabitants of Khirbitā in Egypt and to suppress the chaos which existed in the conquered land . . . until ʿAmr b. al-ʿĀṣ was able to kill him, cut off his head and send it to the house of ʿUthmān b. ʿAffān so that the women of the dead Caliph might dance around the severed jugular vein in a dance of delight at the taking of vengeance.

The tragedy gathered with the death of the struggling Imam ʿAlī b. Abī Ṭālib by a blow from the sword of that stupid traitor. The atmosphere relaxed at the pledging of allegiance to the new Caliph and Muʿāwiya had arrived at kingship.

It is a long chain of sacrifices and endeavours in which Muʿāwiya sprinkled everything which his deliberation made clear to him with an intelligence rarely parallelled in history. In this he used a handful of men around him whom he trained and gave experience to in this same rare intelligence.

ʿAmr b. al-ʿĀṣ responded to his master with every skill in spontaneous improvisation which was ready to face problems and to improvise solutions. He began to drag along the tails of victory at the end of the Battle of Ṣiffīn as if he was a peacock who had every excellence in the colours of his long tail. He did not disdain facing his colleague in the arbitration – Abū Mūsā al-Ashʿarī – with that treachery which did not recognise a single letter in the words, manhood and trust, to the extent that he set himself up as a custodian for the demand for vengeance for ʿUthmān insofar as he did hesitate to murder Muḥammad b. Abī Bakr. Then he compounded that incident with the dreadful crime of cutting off his head.

Al-Mughīra b. Shuʿba began to give solutions for problems, sometimes by giving advice to ʿAlī b. Abī Ṭālib to acknowledge Muʿāwiya's governorship over Syria until the situation quietened down and then he could dismiss him when the circumstances allowed – he gave this advice on the evening of the death of ʿUthmān. Then he changed his view about it in the morning and accepted that it was correct to dismiss the rebel from his position in accordance with the policy of cleaning up the state. Then he went to Mecca to participate in the organisation of the Battle of the Camel and to study how he could gain advantage from the Muslims striking against each other. After that he withdrew to where he continued giving advice but now to

Muᶜāwiya and he helped organise the plots around the actions of the arbitration.

At the time Ziyād, the son of his father, remained in the Eastern theatre of war, gathering together the outposts of the empire in order to wrap them up in obedience to his brother-to-be with that concern and worldly experience which made him aware of everything.

This is a short survey of the long story, all the phases and chapters of which concern Muᶜāwiya b. Abī Sufyān, the instigator of conquests on the Byzantine front, the founder of the Umayyad state and the one who first laid the foundation stone in the division between Kūfa and Damascus, by using tribes from Yemen to help him against tribes from Qays and by employing that intelligence which continued to respond to him throughout the eighty-nine years of his life.

The second front, which had hesitated to fight and was under the command of the new Caliph, began to receive blows to its wide breasts. What do you think that ᶜAlī b. Abī Ṭālib would do? Would he fight against intelligence with intelligence? With what kind of intelligence would he fight?

It is certain that he would not resort to that kind of intelligence which existed in corruption and rottenness. He has said: "By God, Muᶜāwiya is not more intelligent than I am but he is treacherous and sinful. . . . If I had not hated treachery, I could have been the most intelligent of the people in that way. By God, I would not gain advantage through conspiracies and I would not turn away from hardship."

The intelligence which ᶜAlī had was of the pure kind because it was the product of that deliberation which kept away from men's immediate horizons.

The first and last question must be: Why did the people of the world join forces against him if they were not possessed of an obstinate refractory rivalry? Had he threatened them with bringing back tyranny to its place or restoring falsehood? "Your pledge of allegiance to me was not a chance affair." "My affair and your affair are one." "I want you for the sake of God but you want me for the sake of yourselves." "Help me to help yourselves." "I swear by God, I will give justice to the oppressed from their oppressor and I will take the oppressor to his coffers so that I may bring him to the watering-place of truth, even though he is unwilling."

It was natural that the people of the world should resort to defending their interest by that contradictory kind of heroism. It was clear that ᶜAlī b. Abī Ṭālib would confront them with that positive heroism. It was certain that he would gain on every front because he was struggling with the sword of right and the sword of right cannot be broken.

In this way did the intelligence of ᶜAlī b. Abī Ṭālib stand. . . . In this way did deliberation become clear in it. His intelligence was the intelligence of illuminating reason. His deliberation was the deliberation of discerning reason. From this his long-term estimation was that gain could only really be attained in the last stage whose scope would never merely be the span of life on earth, nor even the span of an epoch. Indeed the fact is that all generations will become one broad expanse around which the great truth will circle. Thus the circle which was before him was one in which he would never use a weapon of short-term profit. Indeed what understanding has a man who presents the Message as a model and an ideal? He would never bargain with right, goodness and beauty. How could such a man exchange the abundant for the paltry, the noble for the insignificant? Such a man would never accept the advice of al-Mughīra b. Shuᶜba: "Confirm Muᶜāwiya in his governorship and confirm the other governors in their governorships so that after you have received their obedience and the pledge of allegiance from their soldiers, you could change them and abandon them." He could not do such a thing because he only came to government to purify it. Death was easier for him than denying his principles. He had refused government as limited by ᶜAbd al-Raḥmān b. ᶜAwf and he would never cling on to it at any time when it was connected with bargaining over principles.

As for the intelligent man who claimed that he was qualified to solve problems, he may have presented a solution to the problem of the hour. Yet it was not an absolute solution to the problem of the caliphate in its broadest definition, which required that subjects be treated with right and justice, not that they be treated with oppression and selfishness.

The community was in universal need of a firm structure so that it should not be lost amid clouds and dust and sand. Yet ᶜAlī would never resort to treachery and deceit in order to gain the throne even if that required him to turn away from the caliphate.

Thus through his refusing such advice, the intelligence of ᶜAlī was of the exalted kind which is content to suffer hardship in order to accomplish principles. Similarly he would never have raised copies of the Qur'ān at the Battle of Ṣiffīn in order to deceive any more than he would have been able to exalt his own rank because he, himself, had been for thirty years – and was still – protecting the community and preparing it for such a spurious show as the arbitration. On that day through his acceptance of the treachery he was the first to respond by entrusting the arbitration to the noble pages of the Qur'ān. He was the man most aware of what had come down in the verses of the noble Book. He was the one who said: "Ask me about the Book of God. . . . By God there is not a single verse but I know whether it was revealed at night or during the day, on flat land or in a mountain."

Treachery will melt with the traitor while the document with its noble pages will continue to throb with respect for the one who was betrayed because of his regard for the Noble Book. As the improvisation of the traitor dwindles to the level of his dwarfish reason, the deliberation of the one who was betrayed will be elevated to the peak of its aim.

There was a vast difference between ᶜAmr. b. al-ᶜĀṣ who negotiated with al-Muqawwas about Egypt through the black leader, ᶜUbāda b. al-Ṣāmit, when he said these words: "This black man is one of our lords, one of our best men and one of the foremost among us." . . . and between ᶜAmr b. al-ᶜĀṣ when he was using all his intelligence to get hold of the tribute paid by Egypt by holding the view that the conquest was a cow to be milked. There was a considerable difference between ᶜAmr b. al-ᶜAṣ when he built a mosque in al-Fuṣṭāṭ and ᶜAmr b. al-ᶜĀṣ when he carried a copy of the Qur'ān at the Battle of Ṣiffīn. At one time the Book was the page of faith while at the other time the Book was transformed by him into an outburst of trickery and falsehood.

Where is the improvisation which responds to reason? Where is the intelligence which lives for an hour and then commits suicide? Thus intelligence was going around two pivots in the struggle which broke out between ᶜAlī b. Abī Ṭālib and Muᶜāwiya b. Abī Sufyān. The one intelligence unrolled the shirt of ᶜUthmān wrapped with copies of the Qur'ān while the other intelligence unrolled the copies of the Qur'ān which were rolled in the cloak of the Prophet. One intelligence rests on a bed of silk and brocade while the other intelligence is satisfied with a bed of palm leaves. One intelligence gathers existence in the folds of its shawls while the other intelligence makes room for existence in the pleasant heights of its hills.

The difference between one intelligence and the other intelligence is that one of them continues to jump between generations so that man can be endowed with it in order to achieve the value of man.

Words of Muᶜāwiya b. Abī Sufyān

O awesome creature, let us begin by assessing the two pillars of your life. In the period of ignorance, you used to humble yourself to stone idols and you came to a religion which humbled the earth with you in it to heaven. You were in an age locked in upon itself which lapped up a contaminated civilisation and you were introduced by your new religion to horizons whose civilisations were impregnated with a new light. On the one hand, small tribal grouping gave you support, with which you plunged into limited raids whose purpose was no more than the securing of a livelihood. On the other hand, tribalism came to your support in the much broader conquests, in which all the tribes of the Arabian Peninsula were fused into one to carry the thought and spirit of the Message to the furthest extent. You were in Mecca with your tent with its tent pegs giving you protection against the heat of the noonday sun and you became a power over vast distances with castles, fortresses and escorts.

You were small – please forgive me for saying it! You became great by virtue of the Message. It is not possible for you to be ignorant of that for it was one of the things which you could be praised for. In this way did the splendour of the conquest affect you.

Since the conquest was an operation which aimed at the circulation of the ideas of the Message over all horizons and at the reformation of work by the trends of its spirit and its principles, this is what you were urged to carry out by unsheathing your sword so that it would lay your path to wherever you carried the thoughts and spirit of the Message.

Syria received you as a guide and a raider. It considered the oil of your torch to be of the kind which is purified and perfumed and it found in it a beloved kinsman. Everything in you radiated kinship . . . from blood to ideas, to spirit . . . from desert to desert . . . from neighbourhood to neighbourhood, from a new-comer to an old settler, from one link to another link. With that friendly welcome, Syria received you through the bishop, Manṣūr b. Sergius and his offspring, Saint John of Damascus. If you had come as a raider, it would have only received you as a raider. It only extended degrees of kinship to you because you came with the torch of salvation to save it from the night of conquest. Indeed you only came as a kinsman and a relative.

You did not come as a foreign conqueror. You came as a torch and a light much more than you came as a sword and a shield.

Here the value of the conquest was in front of you, radiating from your Qur'ān to the blade of your sword but not radiating from the tip of your sword to the cover of your Qur'ān. You came to unite. You did not come to separate. There was accomplished at your hand what the Message wanted to be accomplished. Your glory was united with the glory of your people. There was nothing separating you as governor and ᶜUmar b. al-Khaṭṭāb as caliph which even detracts the measure of a fingertip from your value. You and ᶜUmar b. al-Khaṭṭāb were two pivots in the field of glory and a struggle which bound together Syria and Medina with a bond which was firm in contact. The bond which bound the Arabian Peninsula to Kūfa could only borrow its firmness from your bond which tied the threads to every Muslim fighter with the sinews of his religion rather than with the members of his tribe.

At that time you could be characterised by intelligence since you were guided to it by good deliberation. There is no doubt that with these great qualities you could have founded a throne for Syria which outstripped the thrones of Byzantium at the greatest period of their glory even though its glories would not have been for you. For you were only the master of what was due to you and you were an ordinary fighter.

It could not be accomplished by the power of the tribe of Kalb alone without the tribes of Qays also extending the hand of friendship. Nor would the tribes of Kalb and Qays have been able to achieve it unless they had been all fused together in a new crucible. The new crucible was that which gave the sword its splendour, gave the struggle its spirit, gave the aims their beliefs and gave the programme its philosophy. . . . What programme can there be without a philosophy to set rights its outlines, to construct its aims and to settle its different aspects? When are lands established for the world itself? When is sweet water made pure for it? . . . except to the extent of the springs of virtues which it drinks from and the fountains of beauty at which it refreshes itself.

This or that are both the spirit which emanates from the new Message which was a new crucible for the new Arabian Peninsula so that a new conquest burst forth with that Message.

Muᶜāwiya, through the abundance of your deliberation, you were aware that, when the Arabian Peninsula was unified, it would achieve that miracle. Similarly you were aware that at no time in its history had it ever been unified like it had been unified then. The secret of its unity could not have remained hidden to you. Yet despite that, you rode roughshod over it in order to achieve victory for the family of Umayya over the family of Hāshim. As a result you banished the certain victory of the Message.

The victory of the family of Umayya and the victory of the family of Hāshim became your true victory when you were stripping Syria of its mixture of foreigners and when your brother was cleansing Iraq of Persians. [The author must mean by 'foreigners' and 'Persians' here the unbelieving rulers whose influence had extended to Syria and Iraq through the emperors of Byzantium and Persia. 'Foreigner' in its national or regional sense is not considered a foreigner in the Islamic purification of evil. (*Note inserted by the Committee*)]

Syria and Iraq were your two freed wings in your great world.

What harm would there have been to you if you had stretched out your hand to ʿAlī b. Abī Ṭālib so that your two palms were joined for united benefit? You knew with absolute knowledge that your cousin had clean hands because he had a clean heart, reason and spirit. You were not absolutely ignorant of the fact that he was the great pivot around which the pivot of the Message circulated while you were laying paths to power for yourself with it. You knew that he was the firm foundation for all your fortresses which had sprung up and that he had every right to struggle and every right to precedence. To him the merit of the programme and its execution refers; through him relatives are protected; to him directions point because he is the pure and chaste, the man with great knowledge and the zealous proof of all the roots of logic. Indeed he is the true test, the wise leader and the determined hero.

Was anything better for you than to join your breast to his heart and your judgment to his wisdom? Then your world would drink his religion and your intelligence would be polished by his judiciousness. Then your world would be sound in all its aspects and firm in all its moulds. What benefit to the world is it that the eminence of divine laws evades it and it is devoid of the garb of virtues?

If it had been possible for you to see everything which happened after you left the world, you would have been the first to be sorry and the most intense in regret.

The slaughtering blazed forth in civil wars throughout the land which stretched from the Persian Gulf to the Dead Sea. More than one rose up to demand the caliphate for himself until finally he fell dead amid a scene of tumult with tens of thousands around him, all of them sprung from the roots of the tribes of Qaḥṭān and ᶜAdnān, sometimes killed in al-Ḥīra, sometimes in Baṣra, sometimes even in Mecca and the Kaᶜba and sometimes in Kūfa.

Thus was civil discord rapidly transported from Syria to Iraq, or from Syria to Egypt, or to Egypt, Iraq and Syria at one time.

No slaughtering was more generous than it in cutting off the heads of thousands and in the many different kinds of persecution and torture which were coloured by different techniques . . . including treachery, assassination and poisoning.

[Just before this description the author has mentioned that if it had been possible for Muᶜāwiya to see what happened, he would have regretted. Indeed it should be rather that if it had been possible for him to see what had happened, he would not have regretted his excesses and he would not have hesitated for a moment to carry out his terrible plots which destroyed all or most of the gains of the Islamic experiment. How could he be concerned about hesitating in his activity when he already was aware of the depth of the apostolic tragedy which his plots were bringing about while he was planning and aiming at it in his activity? His own personal glory was not his only concern but rather he was concerned as well with the destruction of the glory and the continuation of the Message. The author should have taken note of the words of Muᶜāwiya in this connection. (*Note inserted by the Committee*)].

Al-Ḥajjāj b. Yūsuf was one of the most outstanding and most powerful figures among the initiators of oppression. He did not keep it in Iraq and he never ceased from carrying it out.

Let the glory of the Arabian Peninsula finally dwindle and become shrunken. Let its sons become scattered as they flee from oppression, tyranny and persecution. Let hatred increase in their hearts and let chains surround their spirits, from one tribe to another, from one side to another and from one generation to another.

The chain of assassinations has not ended. . . . It did not stop at ᶜUthmān b. ᶜAffān, or ᶜAlī b. Abī Ṭālib, or al-Ḥasan b. ᶜAlī. . . . It went on to al-Ḥusayn b. ᶜAlī, to ᶜAbd Allāh b. al-Zubayr, to Marwān b. al-Ḥakam, to al-Walīd b. Yazīd to Marwān b. Muḥammad . . . .

Thus after nine decades Damascus lost your great throne and the bounty of your radiant shelter. Nothing remained to it which would remind it of your epoch except the vast broad mosque to which it took safe refuge.

Thus, Muᶜāwiya, did the world move East with the rising sun and disappearing with its setting so that only the face of your noble Lord abides both before and after?

It was to such minarets as those that ᶜAlī b. Abī Ṭālib was summoning you to pay little heed to the world and to seek unity with the spirit.

It is a duty to scatter virtues over society so that it can, under their protection, enjoy the world without the spectre of apprehension, without hatred and malevolence, without cunning and deviation. That could not be achieved for Arab societies in the lap of a Bedouinism which could not assess characteristics and qualities properly. So it began to be distracted by hatreds and tribal fanaticism. From the period in which its tribalism had been overcome and in which it had achieved the greatest conquests, it did not take a sufficient lesson which would make it rely on the causes of its unity and the secret of its success. Thus it soon returned to the things which caused its collapse.

Who was responsible to give this kind of true education to society except its leaders and rulers? However, the methods by which the rulers treated their subjects were not capable of bringing about harmony. This was an error of sound administration because rivalry for leadership and to occupy important positions in order to gain wide enjoyment of the world was not its concern. That would only be to be concerned to achieve temporary success by appealing to tribalism through enticement with the wealth which poured from the conquests.

So the conquest was corrupted, the rulers were corrupted and society was corrupted. Resorting to violence was the quickest way to achieve the perpetuation of domination and the enjoyment of it. In this way did the whirlpool revolve around itself so that it, itself, began to gnaw into itself.

After your final rest, ᶜAbd Allāh b. al-Zubayr arose to urge al-Ḥusayn b. ᶜAlī to seek his right to govern but the former refrained from giving him any help so that the skies would be free for himself to try to gain power later. The response of your son, Yazīd was to torture al-Ḥusayn, to cut off his head and to offer it to al-Ḥusayn's own sister as a sweet gift so that she could take it back to Karbalā'. Thus a new cry arose for the Shīᶜa, which has not ceased to ring out even today, demanding vengeance for al-Ḥusayn. This gave ᶜAbd Allāh b. al-Zubayr, the so-called helper who himself aspired to the caliphate, an opportunity pregnant with hatred. . . . He achieved the caliphate for himself for a period of nine years and with it he brought about a second Ṣiffīn on all the Arab tribes.

As for Marwān b. al-Ḥakam, that was the chance which he had been waiting for. He took over the caliphate in the name of the Marwānid state after the death of your grandson, Muʿāwiya the Second. He continued to show preference to the tribes of Yemen over the tribes of Qays until ʿĀtika, the mother of Khālid, killed him in the most abominable way.

Al-Ḥajjāj b. Yūsuf headed for Kūfa to say: "Indeed I see heads which have grown ripe and the time for whose harvesting has come. I am the man to do it to them. It is as if I was already looking at the blood flowing between their turbans and beards."

I have tried to count the number of heads which were cut off during that period and their total reached one hundred and twenty thousand.

After you, all this slaughter accompanied every stage of the Umayyad caliphate. In that period hatred, malevolence and trickery took root. During it no attempt at affection, love and tolerance was made which could remove their effects and lighten the weight of their burdens.

Throughout this time, which did not go beyond seventy years, hatred continued to grow and gather to itself a circle in which, from time to time and from caliphate to caliphate, the hearts of men were engulfed and to which their minds paid attention. Thus al-Saffāḥ, the ʿAbbāsid Caliph, took advantage of the opportunity and torture was meted out under him as vengeance for vengeance and torment for torment. Those who had been the flow of the tide now became its ebb and those who had been its ebb now became its flow.

O son of the Umayyad family, in this way you see how the span of time, during which the shirt of ʿUthmān throbbed, has stained the whole epoch with the blood of hundreds of thousands from every Arab tribe. The conquest atrophied in a shameful way to the extent that tribute came to be paid instead of being received. The seat of the caliphate had begun to circulate between Medina and Kūfa, between Kūfa and Syria and between Syria and Baghdad. The tribes themselves, continued to fight each other and shame moved from one front to another and from one age to another. Yet the Caliphs remained in their usual way of life and luxury, exploiting the money due to the Muslims and spending it on their own whims and pleasures, which reached the very limit of depravity and madness.

The people remained sunk in their continuous decline which was far away from true thinking, and a culture which came from the roots of love, goodness and beauty. They did not set up any initiative for a properly directed economy which would make the Arabian Peninsula concentrate on some kind of stability. This was necessary, first and last, in order to fashion the state in a precise manner which would restrict its effort to representing man in the Arabian Peninsula and to producing him in a cultured way. In this way he would become a vigorous force for good before being presented to the clamorous stage on which he had previously been thrown with only his own inability and misfortune.

The first initiative was very weak from the point of view of this basic idea.

O son of the Umayyad family, you began with the shirt of ᶜUthmān by which the scale of the world would tilt towards your breast. So your breast was weighed down by it and the breasts of the men who lived in your time were weighed down by it. You left behind a period which was beaten from side to side by its ebb and flow. Let it be a lesson for the periods which come after it.

ᶜAbd al-Raḥmān b. Muljam

You were not the first to leave the true line of conduct and you will not be the last. You were not the first to carry the burdens of crime and you will not be absolutely the most insignificant of them at the end of time even though the motive in your case was the most stupid and feeble-minded. All men who undertake such an attack carry, like you, this darkness in their souls and this idiotic logic in their heads.

The squalor, which you wallow your body in and into which you put your head, is no less unclean and no less rotten than that in which pigs wallow around decaying garbage in their sties.

What thing can be said about you which is worse than what can be said about any other criminal, you bearer of crime? What concern do you have for the most offensive epithets which can be used against you while you are without every scruple by which even the behaviour of a snake is affected?

However, words about you which do not take care to be used with restraint, will only serve to attack you more than they will serve to attack the crime which was shockingly carried out by you. It was the crime of the epoch which you gulped down as a deadly poison which you had poured on to the tip of your sword. You are the unique perpetrator of the crime. Through you, subterranean stores of hatred against such stupidity have been gathered together.

Some men have said that a woman who wanted vengeance tempted you with her beauty and offered to give herself to you as your price when the required act of bravery was performed for her.

What beauty is this which you felt in the darkness of your soul so that the heat of its flames made use of you? It is nothing but the beauty of the bats which can only be seen in the dark recesses of caves. Yet they have impudently called you a leader . . . when you were able to murder a hero whose like the Arabian Peninsula has never witnessed in its history, neither past nor present.

What heroism is this whose sword you sharpened on two whetstones, the whetstone of poison and the whetstone of assassination? The assassination itself was of the cowardly kind whose previous attempts had failed. It was the poison alone which worked.

In their ignorance they attributed to you the quality of rescuer since you intended that the community should be saved from the originator of its woes and the instigator of its wars.

Shame on you and shame on those who are ignorant like you!

His was a long life of struggle to remove injustice from the back of the community and from your back; to free your generation; to defend the ideal model for every generation which would follow your time; to protect the nobility of every man who was ignorant of his humanity like you were; and to demolish the old Arabian Peninsula – your Arabian Peninsula – and to repair it so that it became worthy to be ranked among civilised societies.

Fellow, what do you claim? What do all those behind you claim? What about all those who passed through a long struggle in which ʿAlī b. Abī Ṭālib spent his whole life in discomforts and hardships, in poverty and deprivation, in long nights of sleeplessness and noble yearning.

For the sake of whom was that? Was it for the sake of destroying the community with civil wars or was it for the sake of purifying the community from the dregs of ignorance and decline? Do you think that he was a mad man trying to grab the land in order to shatter it among the lines of the stars? Or do you think that he was a rational man who had come down from heaven in order to cover the area of the earth with its bounty? Do you think that he came to destroy or do you think that he came to build? Do you think that he came to plunder or do you think that came to give? Did he not have the duty of being the custodian of the Message and was not the supervision of it entrusted to him? Or do you think that he guarded property and betrayed his trust? Don't you see that he carried the Message with his sword and through his explanation just as the wind carries the rain to the thirsty areas of your deserts? Did you not see such loftiness under the blow of your treacherous sword, on the way to mosque, which coloured his head with blood and did you not see such loftiness beneath his patched shirt and his armour which he used on the fields of battle and his mended sandals which he put on his feet?

Have you not heard about Ibn ʿAbbās asking about those sandals. . . . "I went in to the Commander of the faithful and he was mending his sandal. I asked what the value of it was. He answered: 'By God, it is more loved by me than commanding you except for the fact that I am upholding right and driving away falsehood.' "

Have you not heard him saying that? Do you not see that through such substantial evidence he is the most glorious and pious of men?

However, you only saw him through spectacles which had been put on your blind eyes. That was the inheritance from your era. But then your age was more culpable than you to the extent that it did not embrace into its arms that great man and it failed in the duty of putting up an impregnable barrier to make it impossible for little men like you to be able to see the mended patch of his sandal.

That would have been tantamount to the era being devoted to its rare men. So the crime against him has been reckoned in the scales of assessment as a failure to be aware of true values and an avoidance of curbing errors. Indeed on an era which was hungry for men, like the era of the period of ignorance itself, the heavens rained down with ʿAlī b. Abī Ṭālib as abundant rain. Then it rejected him so that it could go back to its old ways and depend on the sewer for its water. Of such an age the least which can be said is that it is blind and its slumber still keeps it in darkness.

As for the man who fell prostrate in front of the mosque of Kūfa, the blow of the sword did not cause his death. Men like him who deal with ideas are in the high towers of those ideas where they are in impregnable safety from any earth-bound creature of the kind like ʿAbd al-Raḥmān b. Muljam.

The blow which was struck on the head of this great genius is still considered to be a grievous thrust against the innermost core of human dignity, despite the fact that it achieved nothing except the triviality of his immediate existence. That blow is still regarded as a disgrace to an era which abandoned his rights and left to later generations the honour of appreciating the man whom they had neglected to appreciate. . . . To such an extent has ᶜAlī b. Abī Ṭālib become the broadest oasis to which man hurries to quench his thirst when he gasps to go with him across the ages.

CONCLUSION

"Tomorrow, you will look back to my time and my innermost thoughts will be revealed to you. Then you will recognise me after I have left my position and another has taken my place."

The Setting and the Rising

How can the thought of man recognise you when you have departed from all the chains which used to bind you, from those hammers which shook beneath the blows of your fists? How did the world come to look at you after it had disowned all you had of it like the night disowns the last trace of its blackness before the coming dawn? How did the scenes of struggle begin to look at you after you had left their shiny sword and polished spear?

By my life! The nineteenth day of the month of Ramaḍān was not the only day when you packed your luggage and made your saddle ready for the long journey! You had prepared to mount that glorious vehicle from the first day in which your eyes were inspired by the great flood of truth whose abundance poured over you from the cave of Ḥirā, from the very day while the world bowed its head before you and threw all its power beneath your feet. From that very moment, your footsteps came to be directed toward the ultimate. Immediate matters did not halt them nor did the dross of the foam of superficial matters distract them.

The world was something which you met with a rough hand, from which you shunned with a sniff of your nose and toward which you aimed the secrets of your heart. Today it is something which gazes towards you as if it had realised that you are the most beautiful embroidery for its garments and that you are the freshest cloud, which has passed, in whose atmosphere the damp ground has been made pleasant. You were the most rational of balanced men in holding it back . . . sometimes when avarice held control of it so that it was blocked by it to the point of suffocation and at other times when it became submerged in pride which was binding it only to tear it apart.

You are the bravest man who ever stretched out a hand towards the adorned cheeks of the world, ripped off the fastenings of its veil, entered into its ornamented boudoir and tore the veil away from it.

There was the unveiled face whose powder the sun now exposed. There was the pampered chamber covered with soft veils whose plague-ridden charms were now laid bare. Thus did you make the great image submit and strip away the coverings of imagination so that you might clothe it in a simple chaste dress. Thus did you wipe from its eyes the sickness of temptation and expose it to the light from which the charms of eye-shadow were gathered.

When this world lost its perished bloom under your eyes, it acquired its blazing fire between the palms of your hands. Now it is a path free of gullies, along which travellers might walk in safety urged on by chaste wishes, delightful hope and pure striving. In order to arrive at a gratifying sleep, neither a night of desire nor the reproach of greed disturbed it. The worm-eaten holes of lust did not violate it nor the hollows of temptation. The insects of the night did not disturb its slumber. In it there was no lack of virtues as if they had been tanned into it like a hide. It did not lack noble qualities.

Thus you maintained the borders of the world when you exposed them. You bestowed treasures upon it wherever its treasures were scattered.

Therefore, it began to refer to you on every occasion when it felt that the road had become too crowded for it. In your constitution for it was the trusted source of reference.

Your constitution was that broad outline for all affairs in life, its problems and its passions. You did not treat any matter without probing its depths and throwing light upon it.

You received the Message. Since it was a gift from the light of your great Lord, not a spark of it escaped you but you gathered it all to your mind and your mind radiated with it. You united it with your power. When your breast was as firm in it as the surface of a shield, you began to serve it out and to pour it forth without the serving enfeebling you or the pouring weakening you.

It was as if you were the open sea. The shores would never tire of the flow of your tides. You did not take hold of a great thing without treating it with greatness. You did not deal with a small matter without giving it of every thought. It was as if you were, both at a distance and near, like the light, the perfection of vision, the answer for sight.

Virtues flocked around the fount of your soul interlocked like the lines of caravans are interlocked with one another. They were pulled tight, with harmony of forms, measured rhythm and smoothed ways.

You were the good man of good men as you were the ascetic of ascetics. You kneaded the world with asceticism and you baked it. Then the tables of goodness were opened to the reality of generosity . . . so that when you took the sliced loaf to eat with a grain of salt, every kind of vitality was in it for you. Your loaf was sufficient for you because its dough was from abstinence. You would never grudge anyone else your bread because its flour was the munificence of your abstinence.

You abstained from the world because you did think that it had any lasting shelter nor any permanent power. You saw that its ways were nothing but transitory and you saw that in it man was rapidly travelling towards death and that he was heading towards the lap of his Lord. You saw that virtues were the best ornaments which man gathers in this world, through which he travels with piety and which he leaves with quiet confidence. . . . They are a comfort in life and a sufficiency for death. You saw that sins are the daughters of inconveniences, which corrupt necessities, harbour hatreds and disturb sleep. Man will never have the reality of the ultimate goal in them. Rather they are the refuge of enfeebled reason and the aim of tempted ambitious men and the insatiable starving. . . . They are a trivial objective, a meagre aim which will never build a man conscious of the reality of existence. Rather will they perpetuate for him a source of discomfort in a painful race in which the competition will wear him down and the trickery and deceit will roll him down.

You stretched out your generous arm to impose integrity in the path, truth in speech, frankness in opinion, truth in judgement and justice in administration. You were offering to the traitor virtues which would enrich him, noble deeds which would adorn him, piety which would perfect him, and faith which longed for him.

Your dough is the purified dough. The hand of the sinner had not stretched his fingers towards it. The food from it is blessed food. In it there is nourishment and in it there is consolation. In it there is submission and contentment. In it there is love and magnanimity. In it there is striving against pride and in it there is contemplation against the arrows of fortune. In it there is the wakefulness of consciousness and the splendour of man.

This is the reality of the world which you have left to the world. It is no wonder that the world hungers for your burnt crumbs when its tables have become overcrowded. Nor is it any wonder that it thirsts to drink your drops when its springs have disappeared. The hunger of the world only produces indigestion and its thirst is only satisfied through an abundance. How is it that the food in your dishes does not produce indigestion and your drink does not sink in excess? That is because you are the very taste of the food since you offer the art of eating and the art of drinking.

Thus the world with its generations will never cease to ladle out the perfume from your spices, O noble face which radiates your Lord.